God Chicks

God Chicks

LIVING LIFE AS A 21ST CENTURY WOMAN

HOLLY WAGNER

THOMAS NELSON PUBLISHERS®
Nashville

A Division of Thomas Nelson, Inc.
www.ThomasNelson.com

Note: Scripture citations in this book are from several different versions of the Bible, listed below. When no particular version is cited, the Scripture is a mix of several different versions.

Published in Nashville, Tennessee, by Thomas Nelson, Inc.

Library of Congress Cataloging-in-Publication Data

Wagner, Holly.

God chicks : living life as a twenty-first-century woman / Holly Wagner.

p. cm.

Includes bibliographical references.

ISBN 0-7852-6448-5 (pbk.)

1. Christian women—Religious life. I. Title.

BV4527 .W295 2003

248.8'43—dc21 2002015690

Printed in the United States of America

03 04 05 06 PHX 6 5

This book is dedicated to the God chicks who have come before me. Thank you for being faithful to run your race with excellence.

And the book is also dedicated to the God chicks who are doing their part on the planet right now. I believe heaven and earth are crying out for you and me to take our places.

Let's do it!

contents

just a little note from me . . .

It is no accident that you and I are alive and on the earth at this time in history. What an awesome privilege it is! Some people say, looking back, "Oh, I wish I could have lived back in the good old days" (whenever those were!). Granted, terror is alive and real on the planet . . . but so are we and so are the purposes for which we have been placed here.

I believe the King of heaven is waiting for you and me to take our places on the earth. We have a job to do.

There was a time in ancient history when we, as women, were told that in order to truly be successful as women, we had to see ourselves as goddesses. Then we were told around A.D. 1200 that we were merely chattel, one step above oxen in the grand scheme of things. Then in the 1960s the message began to spread that to truly accomplish our goals, we had to be like a man . . . think like a man (who could?), and dress like a man.

Basically we went from goddess to cow to man. No wonder women could be confused!! Because *not one* of those is true. We are *women,* and that is more than enough! Being a woman is wonderful. As women, we were put on the earth to accomplish so much. Let's discover it!

In this book I will attempt to describe the different aspects of womanhood and encourage you to embrace them. The world honestly needs you and me to take our places on the earth. We are invaluable . . . and more women need to see themselves this way. We don't have to strive or force our way. We just have to confidently walk as we were created.

The reason I am using the term *chick* is not to be disrespectful, but to have a little fun! So c'mon, you amazing God chick. Open your heart to a picture of the woman you were created to be!

God Chicks

We all have the extraordinary
coded within us,
waiting to be released.

– J.L. Houston

CHAPTER ONE

the just b u chick . . .

Everyone has his own specific vocation in life . . . Therein he cannot be replaced, nor can his life be repeated. Thus, everyone's task is as unique as is his specific opportunity to implement it.

—Viktor Frankl

I'm not exactly sure why we women feel the need to waste time trying to be someone else . . . but we have done so and perhaps still do. About ten or twelve years ago, I was trying to figure out exactly what my role on the planet should be (just a little light thinking!). Therefore, to help me on this journey, I thought I should look at other women who were farther along life's journey than I was.

One of the aspects I knew my life would include was being a teacher of the principles of God. So I began looking for women who were already teachers so that I could be like them. At that time, I saw two different older women . . . both were amazing, but very different from me. They were fairly conservative in their dress style, they wore panty hose, and their hair was never messy . . . shoot, it didn't even move! I was determined to be like them because they were successful in their lives, so I bought sedate suits and *boxes* of panty hose (because I can rarely put on a pair without destroying them!) and had my hair styled like those two women. You would die laughing if you had seen me. In fact, my husband quietly shook his head as he watched the wild woman he married become Conservative Cathy.

I imitated these women in their teaching styles, their mannerisms, and their dress—all because I felt that if they were successful, then I needed to become like them. What an idiot I was!! One day as I was wrestling with my fifth pair of panty hose, and I was complaining about the sadistic man (I'm sure it was a man!) who invented them, I heard the Spirit of God laughing at me. (He does laugh, you know!) I felt that God was asking me what I was doing. I assured Him that I was getting dressed so that I could go teach, and I was putting on panty hose because my two heroes wore panty hose and I needed to be like them in order to fulfill my destiny on the earth. The Father quickly assured me that He didn't need me to be like them. They were fine being themselves, and He didn't need anyone else doing their jobs. He did, however, have a job for me to do on the planet, and He would empower me as soon as I was comfortable being who He created me to be.

I am not a dummy (I know . . . all evidence to the contrary, Holly!) so I ditched those panty hose as quickly as I could!! My two heroes were doing a wonderful job fulfilling their purposes on the earth, and I suddenly realized that I served no one when I wasted time trying to be a poor imitation of someone else.

Each of us has a unique role to play at this time in history, and we will play it only by being comfortable in our own skin.

You and I are supposed to learn from those older, wiser, and smarter than we are . . . but we are *not* to try to become them!! Each of us has a unique role to play at this time in history, and we will play it only by being comfortable in our own skin. Other people should inspire me . . . that's good. When I cross over into comparison . . . that's bad because it becomes destructive. I can never be anyone else; I can only be a better me!

Here's my version of cartoonist Jules Feiffer's story . . .

When I was younger, I always wanted to be like Jenny Washington. She was so cool. I tried to walk like Jenny Washington and talk like Jenny Washington. I liked the things that Jenny Washington liked—I even tried to get the classes Jenny Washington had. Then one day I realized that Jenny Washington imitated Danielle Freedman. She walked like Danielle Freedman walked and talked like Danielle Freedman talked. And Danielle Freedman walked and talked like Michelle Carson. So here I was walking and talking like Jenny Washington's version of Danielle Freedman walking and talking like Michelle Carson. And you know who Michelle Carson walked and talked like? Gina Thompson. Gina Thompson!! She's that little geek who always tries to walk and talk like me!

When I work out in the gym, I can't look too closely at the very buff, well-built people around me because I could get depressed! I just take a quick glance to inspire me, and then I focus on the puny weight I am trying to lift!!

Each of us is irreplaceable, one of a kind . . . priceless! And sometimes I wonder if it isn't like a slap in God's face when we refuse who He made us to be and want something else. As I travel the globe and meet thousands of young girls, I feel the pressure of being a role model of sorts (scary thought, I know!). I am quick to point out that although I am willing to be an inspiration to these girls as they live their lives, I challenge them to find out why they are on the earth and to use their own unique gifts in fulfilling that. Just b u, Chick!! We will be effective only when we are being ourselves. This is not to say we shouldn't continually learn from others and grow . . . because we should!

You were put on the planet on purpose. You are not some

accident—no matter what your parents told you. There is something specific you were created to do. When you discover your life mission, then you feel a sense of purpose and begin to feel confident in who you are. So many children (perhaps you too) have been taught they are basically just exploded tadpoles, randomly placed on the earth with no particular purpose in mind. With this kind of teaching out there, it is no wonder a lot of us feel no sense of purpose and don't truly value the life we have been given. And when you don't value your life, then you mess it up with drugs, bad relationships, or a myriad of other negative things. *Your life has value! There is a reason you are on the planet!* I need you to get this . . . can you tell?

I know that my destiny—the reason I was put on the planet—will involve other people, will help others, and will require others. Dr. Martin Luther King Jr. said it like this: "Everyone has the power of greatness—not for fame but greatness, because greatness is determined by service." No one is supposed to be a Lone Ranger. Together we can accomplish great things, but only if each of us likes who she is, knows her purpose, and is confidently committed to fulfilling it. I'm *not* talking about self-centered, self-serving, and self-indulgent confidence, or the confidence that comes from anger. I'm talking about the confidence that comes from a sense of security, the confidence that allows you to help someone else, the confidence that allows you to give to someone else. A woman who truly knows herself can give freely, knowing that it doesn't take anything away from her, because she has plenty on the inside.

King David said it this way: *I am wonderfully made, and I know it full well.* What do you see when you look in the mirror? Do you see someone who is wonderfully made? Do you know it full well? How powerful that is . . . to know that you are wonderfully made!!! Practice saying that in the mirror! There is a singer named Pink who is quite popular these days, and one of her songs goes like this . . .

> I'm a hazard to myself
> Don't let me get me
> I'm my own worst enemy
> It's bad when you annoy yourself
> so irritating
> Don't want to be my friend no more
> I wanna be somebody else . . .

I don't know Pink, and perhaps she is writing these lyrics a little tongue in cheek. But regardless, the message she is communicating to women today is that when she looks in the mirror, she wants to be someone else. You have got to get good at looking in the mirror and liking the girl you see. You are wonderfully made . . . never forget that. When God made you, He threw out the mold. You are one of a kind, precious, and priceless!

So many young women today suffer from eating disorders. They look in the mirror, and rather than seeing an amazing, loved, one-of-a-kind creation, they see a loser. Rather than wanting to live, they want to die. Maybe this is you. I can only encourage you to get some help. Please don't listen to the lie anymore. You are worth something. In fact, your worth is beyond compare. That is the truth. Let the truth rather than the lie speak louder inside you. Go ahead and say it out loud: "I am wonderfully made! I am loved! I have a purpose on the earth!" Let your mind hear you saying it. Then it will start to believe it.

When God made you, He threw out the mold. You are one of a kind, precious, and priceless!

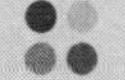

Some people might think that doing this is arrogant, and after all, we are supposed to be humble. Humility is strength under discipline. Only the strong can be humble. Humility is *not* denying who you are. Humility is *not* denying the gifts inside you. Rather, according to my friend Joel Roberts, humility is acknowledging the source of the gift and then giving it fully. Arrogance is failing to deliver the gift given to you. If someone is wounded and bleeding on the side of the road, is humility saying, "Oh, no, not me . . . I can't offer help"? No! Humility is being the one to stop the bleeding if you are the one with the medical training.

Come on, girls. Let's be honest with ourselves. Do you see signs that perhaps you don't know or like who you are created to be? Well, begin the process today! Know that you have a purpose to fulfill on the planet. Purpose can "ignite your spirit, providing personal meaning and deep satisfaction to your life. Purpose is the why—why you are here—and your own special calling. Purpose is the unique gifts and insights that you bring to the planet and can contribute to your world. Purpose fuels your efforts and gives you the drive to continue, no matter what the challenges."[1]

Portraying William Wallace in the movie *Braveheart,* Mel Gibson said, "Every man dies, but not every man really lives." Most people aren't really living their lives with passion and a sense of purpose; instead they are just enduring, waiting, wondering, and hoping something good happens to them. We can't be like that! We should be living our lives with aliveness, excitement, and true joy that we are accomplishing what we are on the planet to accomplish. The world will be a better place when each of us is fulfilling her purpose.

Oprah Winfrey asserted:

> Have the courage to follow your passion—and if you don't know what it is, realize that one reason for your existence on earth is to find it. Your life's work is to find your life's work—and then to exercise the discipline, tenacity, and hard work it takes to pursue it. Do what you love; give it back in the form of service, and you will do more than succeed. You will triumph.[2]

So how do you discover your purpose? There are great books written just to help you figure it out, and there are seminars offered all over the country to encourage you in finding your purpose. So read one or two books and go to a few seminars. But I'll give a few quick pointers here. Discovering your purpose is a process. Ask yourself how you want to be remembered . . . by your husband and your children . . . by your coworkers . . . by your world. Are the things you are doing now leading to that? If not, change what you are doing. If you want to be remembered by your children as a mother who was encouraging, loving, and inspiring, are you being those things now? If you want your community to see you as caring for those who are less fortunate, are you doing that now? What are some words that describe you? What jobs are you doing now? Then list some causes that excite you. These are all things that can help you understand your purpose in each day. Now you set goals that help you accomplish your purpose. Many people set goals and then get frustrated because they don't reach them . . . that's because the goals have very little to do with their purpose, so there is no excitement.

Here's the process. Perhaps you want to be remembered by your community as someone who helped the underdog, as someone who cared for people. And maybe you describe yourself as compassionate, tenderhearted, and a lover of people. Right now, you are teaching kindergarten, and the cause that stirs you is finding a way to make life easier and more fun for children with disabilities. You love to help with Special Olympics and other similar events. Your purpose on the planet will in some way be related to compassionately teaching and helping children who are developmentally disabled. So taking a basket-weaving class may be fun for a moment, but you probably won't finish it because it doesn't relate to your purpose . . . unless you are going to weave baskets for the kids! Set goals that relate to your passion . . . your purpose.

And as you are pursuing that purpose and reaching a goal, you will probably encounter obstacles. Destiny is, after all, a journey—not a destination—and every journey has its obstacles. (Just thought I'd warn you . . . if you haven't encountered any yet!) When you overcome those obstacles, amazing things happen inside you.

Let's say that in order to be healthy and fulfill your destiny, you need to lose one hundred pounds. You begin a diet program and start to exercise because now you see that whether or not you fulfill your destiny can affect all of us. (Remember, we are not Lone Rangers; we need each other!) Losing one hundred pounds is not easy, to say the least. Many obstacles will try to defeat you. Haagen-Dazs still looks good. The gym you joined moves your workout class to 6:00 A.M. instead of the reasonable 8:00 A.M. Your boyfriend breaks up with you, so of course you deserve to eat until you feel better. All of these are obstacles that can sidetrack you from fulfilling your vision. But when you don't allow them to knock you off course and you reach your goal, something happens inside you. You feel amazing. You set a goal and reached it. A lot of people start things, but you actually finished something!

Someone asked me if she should like who she was created to be or who she had become. Actually it is a little of both. I believe

I have been put on the earth to fulfill a mission, and I have been given certain gifts in order to accomplish it. That's the created part. I need to discover my mission, like it, fully embrace it, and at the same time enjoy the gifts in others . . . not waste time coveting them. I enjoy watching amazing women athletes, realizing they are using the gifts given to them. I also love listening to singers who make music come alive. I am neither an athlete nor a singer. (I would fall on my face trying to leave the starting block, and I sing loud and off-key!!) I have discovered the gifts given to me, and I am in the process of figuring out how to grow them. The gifts given to us to fulfill our mission are only in seed form. It then becomes our responsibility to grow them to maturity and thus become the women we were destined to be. It is a lifelong process, so hang in there!

After listening to me teach or watching me lead a women's meeting, women invariably come up to me, often crying, saying, "Thank you for just being you. It has freed me to be me. It feels like a weight has lifted, and it's a whole new day." I have received countless letters from young women who feel that they have been set free to be who they are. One girl said that she didn't know that she could be into karate and skateboarding and be a Bible teacher. She said that just by seeing me, she got hope that she could do the wife, mother, karate, youth-pastor thing . . . all the while being herself. These women may not have gotten deep insights into the prophetic revelations in the book of Revelation (!)—but they left the meeting with the sense that if they were just themselves, amazing things could happen.

Oh, well . . . so I am not the in-depth theology chick . . . and actually that is perfectly okay with me. I will leave that job to someone else! And it is not that I verbally teach the message of being yourself very often, so it is amazing that just by my being comfortable being myself, other women are set free. The same thing will happen in your world when you are just willing to be you.

When you like who you are, you don't spend time wanting what someone else has, or get frustrated and jealous that you don't have the abilities that others do. I heard this true story of a man in South Africa who sold his land and set off to look for diamonds. He knew they had been found in his country, and he wanted to find his share. He traveled all over the country and ended up losing his family and his home in his quest to find diamonds . . . and he found nothing. Meanwhile, the man who had bought *his* land found the largest diamond ever, and the land became the largest diamond-producing area.

How about all of us becoming cheerleaders for each other??!

Too many of us are looking for and wanting the talents and the purposes of others. We spend valuable time wishing we were like someone else, and all the time we have our own treasures inside us . . . just waiting to be discovered. Edwin Elliot said it like this: *By being yourself, you put something wonderful in the world that was not there before!*

We are all supposed to do great things on the earth. And each of us is given different gifts, different tools, with which to do those great things. No one has time to waste being jealous of another. What is with that anyway?? I have been given unique gifts and talents to help me fulfill the purpose I have on the planet. So have you. Your gifts and talents won't help me fulfill my purpose . . . so it's ridiculous for me to want them. Sometimes we girls can be so nasty to each other! (Don't shake your head as if you don't know what I'm talking about!!) We look at someone with a talent and get jealous and mean rather than encouraging her as she runs her race, fulfilling her purpose.

Here's a way to look at it. We are all in the race headed for the finish line. And each is in her own lane. I believe my prize (which is God telling me, "Well done, Holly!") is at the end of my lane. If I were so busy wanting your talents and being jealous of them, then I would actually be trying to run my race from your lane, which would disqualify me. If I got to the finish line in your lane, I could just picture God saying, "Holly, what the heck are you doing here? Your prize isn't here . . . it's in *your* lane!" I certainly *don't* want that to happen. I am not supposed to be jealous of what you have been given. I should be encouraging you with your talents to finish your race.

How about all of us becoming cheerleaders for each other?? Pull out those pom-poms and cheer your friends on. There are some amazing women with amazing talents, and I consider it an honor to be on the planet at the same time they are. Together we will do awesome things for our God, but only if we encourage each other as we fulfill our unique purposes rather than tear each other down by being jealous.

In order to be a b u chick, you must like who you are!! When you like who you are, you are more fun to be around. And one of the ways you know you actually like who you are is that you can laugh at yourself. Recently I was on a stage speaking to hundreds of women, and I thought I was looking pretty cute! I was having a good hair day; I liked the outfit I was wearing . . . a long black skirt, a little black T-shirt with a very colorful halter over it. I'm sure I was in the middle of a life-changing point (?!) when all of a sudden my halter just fell off! (Right when you think you have it all together, something like this happens!) If I hadn't had that little black T-shirt on under the halter, those women would have seen something they hadn't paid for! Was I embarrassed? A little. Did I cry? No. Was I angry? No. Did I leave the stage? No. Have I since learned to tie my halters very tightly? *Yes!* Sometimes things like this happen to us, and instead of laughing, we let the circumstances rob us of our confidence.

In the 1980s I was working as an actress in Los Angeles. One of my first jobs in television was portraying a lead character in a nighttime soap opera (you know, one of those really educational shows!!). I was supposed to be the pretty, young female heartthrob in the show . . . which basically means I was in a bikini or lingerie the entire time! I was a bit nervous because it was my first really big part. As I was being fitted for wardrobe and the different skimpy outfits I would be wearing, the producers decided that my figure was not curvy enough. To remedy this situation, the wardrobe people placed mastectomy pads in my bikini top. (Now you know a Hollywood secret!)

The first scene I was to film involved a conflict between my stepfather and me. We were at the beach, and after our fight, I was to get away from him by running down the beach with my dog. I took off running, and cameras were rolling when one of the mastectomy pads flew out of my bikini top and fell to the sand. I stopped. The dog stopped. I looked at the pad in the sand. The dog looked at the pad in the sand. I knew at that moment that I could have laughed, cried, or been mad at the wardrobe people for not sewing the pad into the bikini top. I chose to laugh.

The director yelled, "Cut!" Wardrobe people came over to remedy the situation . . . which involved a needle and thread! Was I embarrassed? Yes. But because I knew that I am more than my job, I could see the funny side of it. Acting was never my life, only a job. If we would see our lives as more than any singular part of them, we would find it easier to laugh at the mistakes that undoubtedly will come along.

My friend Shanelle, an officer in the United Nations, was flying from one country to another and was seated next to someone she needed to impress. She was speaking very eloquently—and I'm sure she was saying brilliant things—when the flight attendant came by offering Popsicles. Shanelle took one and stuck it in her mouth, not realizing that it had, until recently, been in dry ice. The Popsicle quickly stuck to her lips as she wrapped them around it. She could do nothing! The man she was trying to impress watched as she turned to him with a Popsicle stuck to her mouth. She flagged down the flight attendant and gestured that she was stuck. The flight attendant brought a warm cloth, she put it to her mouth, and the Popsicle was finally released.

It took her a minute to get up the nerve to look the very important man in the face, but eventually she did. She still meets with dignitaries and leaders of countries all over the world. She manages to laugh at herself, knowing that in spite of all the funny, weird stuff that happens, she will accomplish her purpose. Don't take yourself quite so seriously; laugh when you do something silly or when something funny happens. Confident women can . . . and that is your goal: to be a confident just b u chick!

Knowing you were created with a purpose and then overcoming the obstacles on the way to fulfilling that purpose creates an inner strength that comes no other way. And when that strength is there, it allows you to be a just b u chick . . . one who is free to give and free to love . . . and that is our mission on the earth: to love and to give!

Never forget . . .
your value . . .
far above rubies
and pearls.

**– Old Testament, Proverbs 31,
Verse 10**

The royal daughter is all glorious within the palace.

—Old Testament, Psalm 45, verse 13

CHAPTER TWO

the princess chick . . .

Kings' daughters are among

Your honorable women . . .

—OLD TESTAMENT, PSALM 45, VERSE 9

"Once upon a time . . ." is the way most fairy tales start. I like a lot about the romantic fairy tales—the fantasy element and the fact that most of them end with "happily ever after"! And I see nothing wrong with that!!! But I would like to let you know . . . you are a princess, and it is reality . . . it has nothing to do with a fairy tale. And there actually could be a happily ever after . . . it will probably involve work, though! You are a living, breathing, wonderful daughter of the King.

Ezekiel told a story in the Old Testament that paints a vivid picture of how our Creator sees us. In actual fact, Ezekiel was speaking of Jerusalem as he told the story. However, I don't think it is too great a stretch to apply it to you and me.

The story begins . . . *Perhaps when you were born, no one loved you. Perhaps you were abandoned and uncared for on the day of your birth. Maybe no one had compassion on you, and maybe you were even hated.*

There are a number of women I have met around the world who were born in this condition. They were told that they were just an accident, and it would have been better if they had never been born. No one told them they were darling or precious or wonderful or loved. They were left to fend for themselves. They were abused and betrayed by those who should have loved and protected them. That breaks my heart (and, I have to say, it ticks me off!). Maybe this describes you.

> *You are a living, breathing, wonderful daughter of the King.*

And then (the story continues) *in the midst of the pain, your Creator, your Father, comes along and encourages you to live. He commands you to live. He is not afraid of the messes that may surround your life . . . He steps right into them. Then He causes you to grow, to thrive, to mature. He says that He causes your hair to grow and your breasts to mature.* (Well . . . some of us anyway!!!) *He loves you and enters into a covenant with you . . . and then He calls you Mine.*

I just love this. Our Father calls us His . . . Mine . . . that is His name for us. He steps into the messes our lives might be, grows us up . . . calls us beautiful in His eyes. Maybe our lives are messes because of the pain of our pasts . . . or maybe our lives are messes because of some stupid choices we have made. Regardless . . . He enters and calls us His. And the story just gets better!

Then He washes you clean from your past and anoints you for your future. He clothes you in embroidered cloth and puts sandals of badger skin on your feet. (I'm sure they were lovely, although I have scoured the department stores around the country and still haven't found those badger-skin sandals!!!) *He continues to dress you in linen and silk.*

The truth is . . . jeans and a T-shirt would have been fine. But not for our Father. No . . . He wants to dress us like royalty. He sees us as deserving the best.

Then He adorns you with ornaments and bracelets. He puts earrings in your ears and a jewel in your nose. (I'm opting out of that myself . . . but you go ahead with the nose jewel if you want!!) *Then He puts a crown on your head!*

Here's the deal. In spite of the pain and mistakes of your past, God sees you as His daughter . . . calls you His and treats you accordingly. Your past is in the past. Don't let shame cause you to feel ugly. You are anything but!! He commands you to live and not just to live with your head down . . . but to hold it high, wearing the garments of royalty. He calls you beautiful and puts jewels all over you. Then He puts a beautiful crown on your head.

You are a princess because, first, you are a daughter. It is crucial that we girls understand that we are the glorious, delightful, irreplaceable, irresistible, loved-beyond-measure daughters of the King. We *are* His daughters, which makes us princesses.

I won a beauty pageant one time. (Don't hold it against me!!) I must admit that I am not the most graceful of women . . . but I have to say that when the crown was placed on my head, all of a sudden my shoulders went back, my neck grew longer (not sure how!), and I held my head high . . . looking into the horizon. I walked differently because there was this crown on my head.

Most of the pictures I have seen of Princess Diana were of her either helping others in different scenarios around the world or being with her own kids. However, there were some photos of her with her crown on, and I think she, too, walked differently when the crown was on her head. (Maybe it was because hers was real gold and weighed a ton!)

Because we are daughters of the King, you and I have been given a crown . . . let's wear it!!

I am very aware that this idea might be hard for you to accept. I speak to women all over the world who have been taught they were anything *but* a precious daughter or a magnificent princess. For most of their lives, they have been made to feel unworthy, incapable, useless, or at best, average. I have stood on a stage and watched the King of kings use my imperfect words to touch a young girl's heart and give her a different vision of who she is. I have had women come up to me weeping as they thanked me for giving them a picture of who they really are. I am very aware I am just the messenger; I didn't write the psalm or create the image of the princess. I just have the privilege of being one of the women on the earth communicating it at this time in history. And the truth is, I am a girl on a journey, just like you, trying to walk out who I have been created to be.

Here is my friend Mary's story . . .

They say every little girl dreams of being a princess. I just wanted to survive. My childhood, from the beginning, was filled with sadness, feelings of being unwanted, and emptiness. My mother's husband walked out on her, so she took on the responsibility of raising five children as a single mom. The man I longed to call father was a no-show. Between the ages of four and nine I was sexually abused by over five men. At nine I began to have overwhelming thoughts of death.

The thoughts didn't go away as I got older. I didn't believe that I would make it past age eighteen. I became very angry that I was born into this world and thought I would have been better off dead. When I found myself pregnant at eighteen, I didn't think twice about aborting my baby. Why would I put value on my unborn child's life when I put no value on my own?

I continued to seek out love in all the wrong places. Soon, I found myself in a relationship with a man who was twice my age. He told me he loved me and that he wanted to take care of me. It was very appealing to me, because I had never had anyone take care of me. There was no physical abuse, but there was a lot of emotional abuse. He told me regularly that I was not "good enough." I was *never* good enough.

He constantly talked about me having his child. To please him, I did. Three months into the relationship I became pregnant. I then realized that I had made the biggest mistake of my life…not the baby, but rather tying myself to this man. There were a few times I tried to leave, but then I was threatened by the fact that he wouldn't be there for our daughter, just as my father was not there for me. Those words kept me in the relationship for more than four years.

I finally got fed up and so began to make some decisions to change my life. I went to see a counselor, thinking that she could help me work this out. She was very candid. She stated that I was in a very unhealthy relationship that was very controlling. She said that the reason I was in such a relationship was to have the father I never had. Her suggestion was to get out. I prayed that God would show me a way out of this mess.

There was a lady in the neighborhood that had taken me to church for a short period of my life. At this church I remembered hearing how much God loved me and wanted to be my Father. At the time my thoughts were, *Could this be true?* I couldn't understand why my own father didn't love me enough to be a part of my life, so I had some question about the love of a heavenly Father. But I was at such a desperate point in my life; I knew I had to give God a try. I was just determined to give my child a different life. When I made the decision to do things differently, I had an encounter with

God. He began to reveal to me how much He loved me and who He created me to be. He filled that empty void and replaced it with significance. As I learned to forgive myself and forgive those who hurt me, healing for my life began.

Today I am happy to say I have God's best in my life. I am doing things that I never thought I would do. I have so much hope and vision not only for my life and family, but generations to come. Sometimes I can't sleep at night because I am so excited about the things in store for my life. I have the best friends any girl could ask for. I have been married for over eight years to an amazing man!

It's very interesting when I share parts of my story with people, they are shocked. I no longer resemble the girl you read about in the early part of the story. They only see the girl of today...and that girl is full of life!

Today Mary is a healthy, vibrant, successful businesswoman. The God of love reached down to her in the mess she was in, pulled her out, called her His, clothed her in royal robes, and put a crown on her head. She is living her life today knowing that she is an irreplaceable daughter of the King. A princess. So are you.

I love looking at castles . . . mainly because of what I imagine living in one as the princess would have been like. I was in Wales a few years ago and walked through a castle that looked just like the one in the movie *Cinderella*. My imagination went wild!! What would it have been like to be the princess of that castle? (Okay, the truth is probably not nearly as glamorous as my imaginings. I mean, who would want to do the chamber pot thing???) And yet most of us have imagined being Cinderella a time or two . . . and not just the cleaning-up-after-everybody part . . . but the crown-on-the-head, shoe-fitting part! Come on, admit it!!

At one time or another, most of us have played pretend or dress up. My daughter has the most amazing imagination. She can take a towel and a piece of ribbon, and in moments, she becomes a horse with a saddle and bridle. She gets on all fours and whinnies all over the house. The truth is that she loves animals, and while her friends are arguing over who gets to be the mommy or daddy or sisters, she is silent because she just wants to be their horse or their dog. No one ever fights her for those roles!

For a moment, I want you to be that little girl again . . . the one who freely plays dress up. (You don't have to be the horse!) I want you to see yourself as a princess, complete with the crown and robe. Go ahead and buy yourself a tiara and look in the mirror with it on your head. (The Burger King paper one works too . . . I just figured if I'm going to do this, then I want sparkles!!) You need to see yourself with a crown on your head. Why?

When you realize that there is a crown on your head, that you truly are a princess, then you will live your life differently.

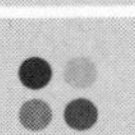

Because that is how God sees you. I just imagine Him looking from heaven and seeing billions of His daughters with crowns on their heads. What a beautiful sight!!

When you realize that there is a crown on your head, that you truly are a princess, then you will live your life differently. You will value your life differently. You tell me: Does a needle in your vein go with the crown on your head? Does giving your body to multiple men go with the crown on your head? Do yelling and hitting your children go with the crown on your head? Does walking around with a permanent scowl or lying to your friend or giving a rude gesture to somebody as you pass him on the freeway go with the crown on your head? Obviously a resounding *no* is the answer to all of these questions. Yet many of us are living our lives every day not realizing that as daughters of the King, we are princesses.

Lisa was just like this . . . unaware of her value. She wrote a letter to me that went something like this . . .

> I walked into the God chick meeting feeling like a woman enslaved, and I walked out a woman filled with hope for the first time in years. I have been sexually promiscuous since college. In college, a baseball player raped me. He had raped several other girls on campus in previous years, but none of us ever turned him in. I guess you could say that this particular incident was my "first time." After that, I blamed myself, got caught up with other "jocks" who forced me to perform certain sexual favors for them, and just decided in my head

that I was destined to live this way. Letting men have their way with me on a regular basis soon made me numb. I was lonely, depressed, and angry. Sex was the only way I could feel loved and wanted by a man for more than five minutes. I was getting drunk regularly and basically just self-destructing. I have never looked at myself as a princess. What woman getting drunk in a bar would? I looked at my life as worthless. Tonight at the God chick meeting, I heard a girl get up and tell her story of choosing to be free from sexual promiscuity. At first I went into shock, then realized that if she could be set free, so could I. For the first time in my life, I feel like I AM a princess and that I CAN be healed and that there IS hope. I know I have only begun the healing process, but I have a goal that one day I will be the girl getting up at the meeting telling her story of victory.

Her victory started when she realized that she is a princess, and she should live her life knowing that. There are too many young women around the world with stories similar to Lisa's. They need to hear the God chick message. They need to know that they are royal daughters. Please live your life knowing it so that you can pass it on!

From the inception of royalty on the earth, kings, queens, and their children were supposed to serve the people they ruled. They were to be the protectors. I'm not sure how this plays out with today's royalty . . . believe it or not, I am not on a first-name basis with any of them! But regardless of whether any of our current royals get this concept of serving or not, you and I must. I am a princess, not to be served, but to serve.

Sometimes I laugh with my friends as I am getting a massage or a manicure or I am eating in a very exclusive restaurant, saying, "I can so-o-o-o do the princess thing!!" One day I was in a wonderful spa, and there were people working on every part of me . . . my back . . . my feet . . . my hands . . . my hair. And I gotta tell you, I loved every minute of it!!

I am a princess, not to be served, but to serve.

I like the finer things in life. Come on . . . who doesn't? And honestly I don't see why I shouldn't have them. I am my Father's daughter, after all! And while I play with my friends about doing the "princess thing," I am not confused about the reason I am a princess on the earth. I am here to serve humanity, not to be served. So are you. But we can serve our fellowman only when we understand our role. When we understand that we are His daughters and thus have access to all that He has, then we can freely serve and freely give.

My friend Robin was homeless at one point in her life. She had been let down by those who should have cared for her. She didn't understand that she was a royal daughter, and so she made some horrible choices that ultimately landed her on the street. She slept where she could and tried to stay clean. Eventually someone extended a helping hand. Now, years later, Robin understands that as a princess, she is to serve humanity. Once a month, with a team of people that she recruited, Princess Robin takes lunches and offers haircuts to the homeless in our city. She sits and has lunch with a woman who lives on the street, not yet knowing her value. And one day, that woman will understand, as Robin did, that she is a princess. She will begin to live her life that way and will then extend her hand to someone else. When we understand our value as daughters of the King, not only will our lives be changed, but so will the life of each person with whom we come in contact.

The world has the princess marketing scheme down. There are images of crowns everywhere. There are hundreds of T-shirts with the word *princess* on them. I think it is time the church puts this princess thing in its proper context. We are not princesses to be served, but to serve. We are representatives of our Father, the King. So put your crown on, Princess, hold your head high, and live your life serving people as a beautiful, without-compare daughter of the King.

> *The bride, the beautiful princess, a royal daughter is glorious. She waits within her chamber, dressed in a gown woven with gold. Wearing the finest garments, she is brought to the King. Her friends, her companions, follow her into the royal palace. What a joyful, enthusiastic, excited procession as they enter the palace! She comes before her King, who is wild for her!*
>
> —Old Testament, Psalm 45

Tiara

Bought from the 2 dollar shop,
Plastic silver
With green and red and blue
Painted on jewels.

But on your head
The most precious thing
in the world.

Prancing and dancing,
Twirling and whirling,
Strutting in front of the mirror.

No narcissistic hang-ups,
Or vain misconceptions.

You hold your head up high,
And tell me you are a princess,
The daughter of a King,

And I believe in you.

—Kathleen Deacon

HEY, WARRIOR PRINCESS . . .

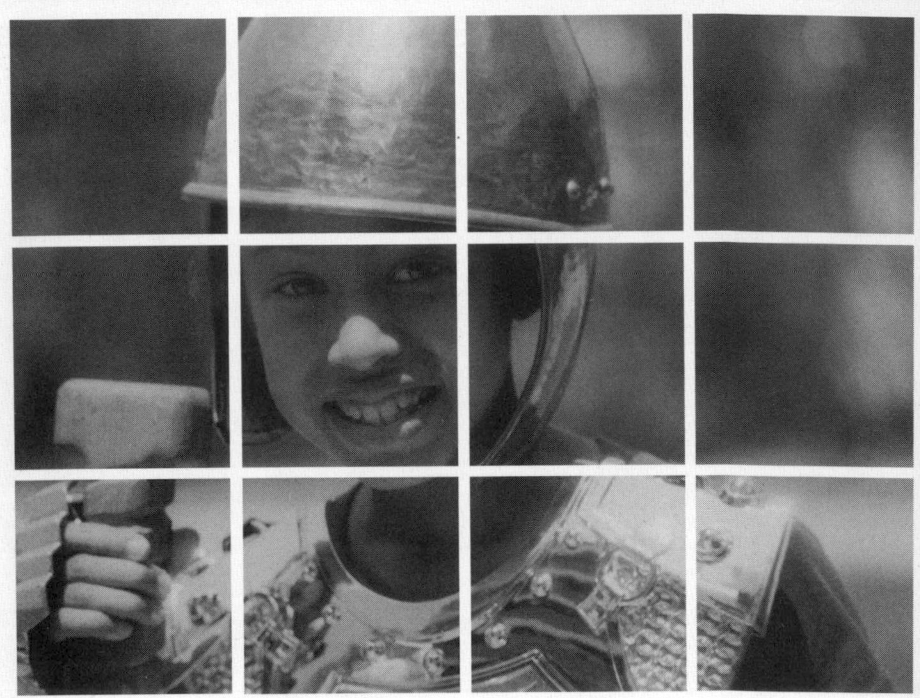

. . . RIDE ON TRIUMPHANTLY FOR THE CAUSE OF TRUTH, MERCY, AND JUSTICE.

—Old Testament, Psalm 45, verse 4

CHAPTER THREE

the warrior chick . . .

Put on your sword, powerful warrior . . .
Win the victory for what is true and right.
Your power will do amazing things.

—Old Testament, Psalm 45, verses 3 and 4 (ncv)

I was not a big fan of the thirty-first chapter of Proverbs . . . mainly because the woman described in this chapter is called the "virtuous woman." In my mind, she sounded like someone who was quiet, weak, wimpy, and did a lot of crocheting! (No offense to all you crocheters out there!!) So I just decided to quit reading it because I couldn't relate to that picture. However, in my quest to become the woman on the earth I was created to be, I kept going back to the girl of Proverbs 31. The truth is, I was intimidated and at the same time just a bit infatuated with her life! I began to spend hours studying her and getting to know who she was . . . and *maybe* on this journey I would find out just a little about who I was to be.

As I was reading about her, I did a study on what the word *virtuous* means . . . I mean, other than my opinion of what the word meant! And to my surprise, I found out that the word *virtuous* means "a force on the earth consisting of three things: people, means, and resource."[1] She is not a wimp, after all!!! She is a warrior! She was created to be a force!!! I could relate to this because I wanted to make an impact on my generation . . . I wanted to be a force on the earth.

All of a sudden, the picture was becoming clearer and very exciting to me. Not only was I a princess, but I was also a warrior! Warrior princess . . . that's me!!

What does it mean to be a warrior? The psalmist told me that I am to win the victory for what is true and right (move over, Joan of Arc!), and ride on triumphantly for the cause of truth, mercy, and justice. That is the reason we are warriors—for a cause bigger than ourselves! (But more about that later.)

The warrior princess has courage.

How do I become this warrior? What are the qualities of a good soldier?

The warrior princess has courage. Too many people I know

are bound up with one fear or another. But if I am to take my place on the earth as a warrior, I must kill the fear and develop courage.

You and I have been given courage . . . and we've been given courage in order to fight the fears that attempt to knock us off course. We have been given courage to finish the journey set before us.

At one point, Ann Landers received about ten thousand letters a week. She was once asked, "What is the most common problem that you are asked to deal with?" She said, "Without a doubt—fear."

This is the age of anxiety . . . so many people are afraid of so many things. But if we let fear rule us, we will remain contained, and we will never realize our potential.

Fear can act like a brake on your life. It stops you from becoming and doing all God wants you to be and do. It limits your potential and hinders your ability to be effective.

When we're afraid, we don't try new ideas because we fear that they will fail or we will be rejected, and so we miss opportunities for success. We are warrior princesses! We need to blast through fear!

A few years ago I began taking karate, and I was determined to get my black belt. It was certainly a difficult challenge I had given myself! There were many times along the journey toward my black belt that I wanted to quit. However, four and a half years after I began karate, I entered the studio to take my black-belt test. I went into that room knowing that at the end of the test, I would have to fight a black belt . . . probably the man who had been a black belt for years. And yes, I was just a little afraid. All through the grueling testing process, in the back of my mind, was the tiny (!) fear that the man I was going to fight could whip my tail!

After I finished two hours of testing, I was told to put on my sparring gear and prepare to fight. Yes, I was afraid. I knew I didn't have to beat him . . . I just had to be willing to fight. As we began to fight, the fear never left me. I just wanted the prize more than I was willing to let the fear stop me. I fought afraid. At the end of the fight, I was presented with my black belt! Yippeeee!! (I'm not sure I took that thing off for days!!)

Sometimes we will feel afraid when we do things. If we let fear stop us, we won't receive the reward. Feel the fear and do it anyway! It is not that the warrior princess is unafraid . . . it is just that she keeps on going!

Every person who ever did anything amazing started out just a bit afraid.

Every person who ever did anything amazing started out just a bit afraid. It is always a risk to try something new . . .

She was spit upon, ridiculed, laughed at, and scorned; she was called a witch and a baby killer. Everywhere she turned, she faced repeated rejections. She lost the man she loved. He, like most men of their generation, did not want a woman who had opinions and thought for herself. He was attracted and at the same time repulsed by her intelligence. She was severely injured and became blind in one eye. She was a woman courageously pioneering her way into an arena solely occupied by men. If it had not been for a desperate plea from a dying friend and a supernatural divine revelation from God, she would surely have quit. But she didn't quit. Instead, against all odds, Elizabeth Blackwell accomplished her dream. In 1847, she entered medical school and became America's first woman doctor. She accomplished her dream by courageously focusing on *why* she was becoming a doctor. At that time in history, poor women virtually had no health care. Many died. She was determined to change that. So when she was ridiculed, when she felt fear from the threats of others, she tapped into the courage we have all been given and rose up as the warrior. Today women of all generations have a lot for which to applaud Elizabeth Blackwell.

Don't let fear keep you small. Don't let fear contain the potential inside you. You are to courageously rise up as a warrior!

How many of you were born in the twentieth century? Well, cars and airplanes became available for mass transportion in this century. Do you think God knew that? Of course . . . and He saw to it that you were born then. If He had wanted you in the time of horses and buggies, you would have been born at another time . . . so He must want you to use airplanes and cars and not be afraid. Many people's potential is paralyzed because they won't get in a car or on an airplane.

Because of the attacks on September 11, more and more people live their lives afraid . . . of airplane crashes . . . of biological warfare . . . of people who look different from them. Many are stocking up on antibiotics or freaking out about the stock market—all motivated by fear. What was your reaction to the events of September 11? Perhaps you reevaluated your priorities. That's good. Maybe you decided to really live your life instead of just existing. That's good. Maybe you decided to pull away from people and hide in fear. That's bad.

Now, I understand the need for wisdom and caution . . . but I refuse to live my life in fear of what may happen! I have too much to do on the earth! Proverbs 31 tells us that the woman each of us is to be rises while it is dark (I initially thought this meant that she rises before the sunrise . . . *yuck*). However, more important than the time of day that we rise is that we rise in the midst of dark times. We are to become strong in the midst of trouble. We are the warriors whose courage rises to the surface when others might be wilting around us.

In the Old Testament, during a time of moral decay, decline, and violence, God raised up a woman to help lead His people. The children of Israel were once again in bondage to a foreign king. God heard their cry and used Deborah to lead them to freedom. She was just a girl, like you and me, given an opportunity to rise in the midst of darkness. She accepted the challenge and encouraged military leaders to victory.

Esther was another woman who rose up courageously in spite of feeling afraid. Even though she was the queen, she was not allowed to see her husband, the king, unless he called for her. However, when she found out that her people were going to be killed, she bravely entered the court of the king on behalf of her people and was willing to lay down her life . . . willing to risk it all. Because of her courage, a nation of people was saved. Yes, she was afraid—but she stepped forward anyway. Why? Because the cause was greater than herself.

By letting fear contain me, it not only limits me—but it could very well hurt others. We need to take the focus off ourselves and be the warriors for a world that so desperately needs to see courage in action.

By letting fear contain me, it not only limits me—but it could very well hurt others.

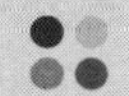

God did that a few times; He raised up a woman in the midst of darkness. I think He is doing it today in the midst of the darkness and fear alive on the planet . . . only not just *a* woman . . . but *the* woman . . . all of us today working together to partner with man to see God's kingdom of love and justice established on the planet.

As the attacks on the World Trade Center were occurring on September 11, 2001, I was on a transpacific flight from Los Angeles to New Zealand. I was headed there to speak at a women's conference. When our plane landed in Auckland, the doors remained closed until someone could come on and tell the passengers about a crisis that occurred while we had been en route. As we listened in horror to what had happened in New York, Pennsylvania, and the Pentagon, tears streamed down many of our faces.

When I got off the plane and realized that I couldn't go home even if I wanted to, I was just a little freaked out! The little girl in me took over. I called my husband and cried that I wanted to come home. He assured me that they (my family) were fine and that I would be fine too. In his own sweet way, he challenged me to rise to the occasion. After I hung up, the warrior in me rose up. I realized that I was in New Zealand for a reason, and my job was to fulfill the mission I had been sent there to accomplish. There will be times when you have to do things you don't want to do, and that is when the warrior must rise up. She is in you.

Lisa Beamer, whose husband, Todd, was killed on September 11, 2001, on Flight 93 when it crashed in Pennsylvania, said that she wanted to make a statement against fear. On October 19, just a little more than a month after her husband was killed, she boarded the same Newark to San Francisco flight that her husband had been on. She did it in an effort to support President Bush's efforts to encourage Americans not to be held captive by terrorism. I'm sure she was feeling all sorts of emotions, but that didn't stop her from doing what she knew was the right thing to do. The warrior in her rose up! Good for you, Lisa!

The Chinese character for crisis is actually the combination of two concepts: opportunity and danger. It is all a matter of how you look at it.

> *Don't let fear control your life's potential.*

There is a story told of two different Vietnam veterans with a similar story. Both were commanders of a unit in which all the men were killed and they were the only survivors. They came back to the United States and had different responses. One decided that losing people hurt too much and so he pulled away from humanity and became a recluse. The other decided that life was short and that he had better take advantage of every moment . . . and so he immersed himself in people and relationships.

Same story—two different reactions. Don't let fear control your life's potential.

You may not realize it, but your fears affect everybody else around you. Your fears influence everybody with whom you relate. Have you ever seen parents ruin kids' lives because of their own fears?

Before Philip and I had children, we were baby-sitting for someone else. (You know . . . getting in lots of practice!) We took the six-year-old girl we were watching to the circus. We got out of our car and walked to the street where we would cross and enter the arena. The girl got very nervous and asked how we were going to cross the street. I told her that we would go to the crosswalk and wait for the light to change. She was still very shaky as we crossed the street. And then I realized that she was afraid, whether it was of cars or of crossing the street I'm not sure. Later that night as I was putting her to bed, she once again became very nervous. She wanted to make sure I had closed and locked all the windows. Where had a six-year-old learned to be afraid of streets and open windows? Her mother. We have to be careful, when we are teaching our children to be cautious, that our own fears are not becoming theirs.

If we are not careful, we can also let fear ruin the very relationships we are created to enjoy. Rick Warren said it like this: fear causes us to cover up. Fear causes us to wear masks. Fear causes us to avoid saying what we're really thinking, to pretend that we're somebody that we're not. It causes us to lie. The greatest block to intimacy in a marriage, a friendship, or any relationship is fear. Why am I afraid to tell you who I am? Because if I tell you who I am, you may not like who I really am, and I'm all I've got. If you don't like me, I'm stuck! So fear causes us to hide, and it ruins relationships. Fearful people cannot give love, and fearful people cannot receive love. Fearful people cannot make commitments to others. Fear cannot allow me to let my hair down and be real.

How many times have you said, "I'm afraid I might get hurt again"? So you don't open up to anyone, therefore limiting your own life . . . and keeping yourself from the relationships that could very well bring you joy. Come on, Warrior chick, have the courage to open your heart again. You need to be wise about whom you open it to, but you do need to open it again!

It takes courage to forgive. And don't wait until you feel like forgiving to forgive because you never will. I never *feel* like forgiving. I usually feel like yelling and hitting, or withdrawing and giving up on the relationship. However, forgiveness doesn't come out of my feelings; it comes out of my will. I will to forgive. I make the choice.

I have to say, when someone hurts me or lies about me, what I want to do is bless that person with a brick! But I have learned that for my life to move forward unhindered, I must be a forgiver.

Forgiveness is man's deepest need and
God's highest achievement.
—HORACE BUSHNELL

The truth is, I have been forgiven much . . . by my Creator when I have made stupid choices . . . by my family when I have let them down . . . by my friends when I have said the wrong thing. Who am I to hold on to unforgiveness when I have been so forgiven?

Offering forgiveness doesn't mean pretending the mistake didn't happen; it means acknowledging it and moving on.

We need to be willing to forgive when someone makes a mistake, says something she shouldn't (that is usually my mistake), forgets to call us back (okay, I've done this too!), is late for the coffee date (oops, guilty again!), doesn't respond the way we think she should, or commits another "crime" against us. Offering forgiveness doesn't mean pretending the mistake didn't happen; it means acknowledging it and moving on.

Don't just open your heart again to be hurt if you haven't talked about what went wrong. One time my friend abandoned me at a moment when I needed her. Rather than pulling away, which is what I wanted to do, I said to her, "If you want to be my friend, you can't do this to me again." I set a boundary with her . . . she couldn't continue to abandon me and be my friend . . . and I still opened my heart to her again, forgiving her and giving her another chance.

Kathryn truly valued her friendship with Natasha. Both have a zest for life and are equally passionate about their individual pursuits. Natasha is older and more experienced in life, and unfortunately she communicated that to Kathryn in some ways that felt degrading. I asked Kathryn about it, and she said, "I felt that at times she would talk down to me, as if I didn't know how to make a decision. I can't help being young or inexperienced. Her daily 'little comments' caused me to withdraw, and I had to make the decision to forgive her or abandon the friendship. I realized the friendship was too valuable for me to break, and so I made the decision to forgive her. And we have a great friendship today." In order to keep the friendship on the right path, Kathryn needed to forgive Natasha, at the same time letting her know that the comments were hurtful, and that she didn't want to be talked down to.

Offering forgiveness means letting go of the offense whether or not the other person says, "I'm sorry." Of course, we all need to be willing to say we're sorry. In fact, go ahead and be the first, but don't wait to start forgiving until the other person says she is sorry too. If you wait for an apology before you begin to forgive, you are putting the power to forgive in the other person's hands when it belongs in yours.

Relationships grow on forgiveness, not perfection. Offenses are going to come, so be ready to forgive. Forgiveness is a way of showing that we accept another's humanity. I believe there are certain relationships I need to maintain and build in order for me to accomplish the mission I have been put on the earth to accomplish, so I can't just give up on a friend when she does something stupid (and no one is exempt from doing stupid things from time to time).

I believe forgiveness is a life-and-death issue.

Forgiveness isn't just a nice thing to do. I believe it is a life-and-death issue. I remember talking with a man who had a life threatening illness. This very ill man was extremely angry with someone who owed him three hundred dollars. It didn't appear he was going to get his money back, and he was furious, shaking his fists and going red in the face. When I suggested that he go ahead and forgive the debt and the debtor since it didn't look as if he was going to be paid back, he became even more angry. Should the debtor have paid his debts? Absolutely. Did the lender deserve to get his money back? Yes. Was it worth his life? I don't think so. I believe the bitterness inside him was killing him.

I have known people dying of cancer or struggling with ulcers who refuse to forgive someone who owes them something, or someone who has betrayed them. They are literally eaten up on the inside with unforgiveness.

Forgiveness takes courage and can be difficult for us because it pulls against our concept of justice. We want revenge for offenses suffered. (Oh, sometimes we won't admit it, but we do!) We want God to bless the offenders with a lightning bolt! You may ask, "Why should I let them off the hook?" That's the problem: as long as you are holding back forgiveness, you're hooked. Or you may say, "You don't understand how much they hurt me!" But don't you see? They are still hurting you. You are still living the betrayal, the offense, whatever the crime. You don't forgive another person for *his* sake; you do it for *your* sake so that you can be free . . . free to love, free to be at peace, free to enjoy the day without being eaten up on the inside.

Being forgiving is not necessarily forgetting. If someone has betrayed me, I am going to choose to forgive, but I will not just immediately open my whole heart again. I might give her a piece to see if she can be trusted with that.

Jesus, King of forgiveness, told us that in the same way we forgive, we will be forgiven. I'm pretty sure I am not finished making mistakes, so if I want forgiveness, I had better be quick to forgive!

C'mon, girls, let's be ready, courageous, and willing to forgive each other. Let's not grow up to be little old ladies so full of bitterness that we are drags to be around.

I wonder if most hospitals—psychological and medical—would be practically emptied if people could truly forgive . . . themselves for the crimes they committed and others for what was perpetrated against them.

I wonder whether most wars and other injustices would cease if we could all truly forgive. Just a thought.

A warrior chick knows how to handle fear and has the courage to forgive. I believe that another aspect of being a warrior involves staying at the post to which you have been assigned. In a real war, soldiers must stay at their positions in order to achieve victory. The pilots dropping bombs over Berlin in World War II stayed at their posts even when the antiaircraft guns were being shot at them. The firefighters in New York City on September 11 stayed at their posts even when buildings were falling.

Another aspect of being a warrior involves staying at the post to which you have been assigned.

One of my posts is that of a wife. So, even if Philip and I have a serious disagreement and I am not a happy soldier, and Mr. Universe walks by quoting Shakespeare, I'm not distracted. I know that my post is next to Philip forever. Another of my posts is that of a mother, so I train my children and love them, even though there are times I want to send them far, far away!! I am committed to that post. Another of my posts is that of a teacher, so I spend time training my mind, going to conferences, and studying so that I can continually improve. I am also a friend, so I invest time in people, even when I may prefer to be alone. I am determined to stay at the posts in my life. What posts do you have?

A warrior is also willing to die for the cause. This certainly was evident on September 11. And perhaps there will come a time when you must be willing to give your life for a cause greater than yourself. Martin Luther King Jr. went into his battle willing to give up his life for the cause, and in fact, he did.

Jineth Bedoya Lima is known as a warrior for free speech. She is a reporter for the daily *El Espectador* in Bogotá, Colombia. On May 25, 2000, she was kidnapped while waiting to interview members of a paramilitary group outside a Bogotá prison. She was raped and tortured. A taxi driver found her at a roadside garbage dump that evening. Jineth is unstoppable. Within two weeks of the attack, she was back at her job, reporting. The International Women's Media Foundation recognized her in 2001 with a Courage in Journalism Award, and upon accepting the award, Jineth said, "They can silence me and kill me and torture me, but there will always be someone willing to expose the truth."[2]

Florence Nightingale, who volunteered to be a nurse on the battlefield knowing she might die, has been quoted as saying,

"You ask me why I do not write something . . . I think one's feelings waste themselves in words. They ought all to be distilled into actions and into actions which bring results." However, I'm not sure we will be asked very often to give up our physical lives . . . but perhaps our egos.

Our egos are not sacred. We need to be willing to lay aside our rights and perhaps our desires in order to achieve the greater good. Be courageous . . . be the first to say, "I'm sorry." Be courageous . . . love your enemies. Be courageous . . . choose a friend outside your culture. Be courageous . . . tell the truth instead of the lie that might want to spring to your lips. Be courageous . . . stay committed to the path of love even when it is hard. Be courageous . . . respect authority. (Let me tell you a story about that!)

I met Shanelle about ten years ago while she was attending the University of Southern California. She is a very intelligent woman and soon graduated with an engineering degree. After she had been working for a few months at her first job, which she had been thrilled to get, she came to me complaining about her boss. She claimed that she knew more than he did. He was too hard to work for and didn't listen to her ideas. He never admitted when he was wrong, which was often, nor did he give her credit for good ideas she had come up with. She didn't think she could take it anymore. I agreed with her that it sounded like a difficult situation, and then I asked her if she wanted some help in dealing with it. She replied, "Yes." Our conversation basically went something like this:

"Shanelle, do you believe this is the job that will use your skills effectively?"

"Yes."

"Are there still things you can learn from this company?"

"Yes."

"What do you think your job is as an employee?"

"I guess it's to do the work I am asked to do and do it well."

"Are you doing that?"

"Well, my boss makes it so hard!"

"Who said life was easy?? Your job as his employee is to learn from him, to be a good representative of him, to adapt yourself to his requirements . . . obviously nothing immoral! . . . and to be faithful to do good work . . . that is, if you want a promotion."

She assured me that she did want to advance in the company and that she was willing to make some changes in her attitude. It wasn't an easy task, but she began to yield to her boss and be supportive. She quit complaining about him and began to do the work he asked without having an "I know better" attitude. (In many instances she did know better . . . that was what made it a real challenge!) In a short span of years, she was promoted to vice president of her company, where she was the highest-paid woman executive.

At every level along the way people saw how hard she worked, for whomever her boss was, and so they kept promoting her. She even bypassed her initial boss. She was promoted time and again over other men and women who didn't understand this concept. She wasn't a doormat. She expressed her opinions whenever they were requested. She was promoted over men and women who were trying to fight their way to the top, complaining about their bosses all the way. She learned to respect the position of boss, whether she ever respected the person as an individual. She continued to find favor within the company and with her clients all over the world.

Now, I believe, as a direct result of her understanding this concept, she was offered and she accepted a position as an officer in the United Nations, where she has had global influence. She went from being a frustrated low-level engineer to one of the most influential women in an organization of worldwide importance, spending her time with presidents and heads of state.

She courageously laid down her ego, and I believe God rewarded her. I actually think that when we are willing to lay down our rights, then God begins to fight for us.

As a daughter of the King, I know that blessing and abundance are promised to me. But that doesn't mean I won't have to fight some battles to obtain what's been promised! God promised the children of Israel that He would lead them into a land "flowing with milk and honey." Sounds good to me! However, they didn't just walk into the land and start drinking the milk. They had some battles to fight. Their first challenge was the slight problem of Jericho . . . a huge, well-protected city. They couldn't go in, knock on the gate, and say, "God told us this land is ours, so you will have to get out." No, it was a little more involved than that!

They did get victory over Jericho and went on to the next city, which was a small one called Ai. Because they had defeated the giant of Jericho, they decided they could send in the second string to defeat Ai. However, they lost their first battle with Ai because someone in their camp had not obeyed God's direction. Perhaps they thought that since Ai was so small, they could fight the battle without God. Big mistake!!

So, yes, there will be battles we have to fight as we move to take our *promised land* (battles that probably don't involve swords and knives!), but let's not make the mistake of thinking we will be successful without God. In the next chapter, I will talk about some of the obstacles we must conquer. Battles are much easier to fight when He is on our side!

"Okay," I can hear you saying to me, "you want us to be fighters."

Well, yes, the warrior chick knows there are some battles she must fight . . . the battle to reach her dreams, the battle to forgive, the battle to stay at her post, and the battle to lay down her ego. The warrior chick also knows how to handle the conflicts that arise with people. And she knows how to handle those conflicts without hurting people.

In any relationship, conflicts will arise. What do you do when your husband hurts your feelings? What do you do when you see something in your friend that can ultimately destroy the friendship? Can you agree to disagree, or do you let the disagreement cause you to pull away?

Some of us may have been raised in homes where any conflict was an abusive one, where all disagreements got out of hand. But it doesn't have to be like that. And the truth is, I never know what kind of relationship I have until we manage to survive a rough patch. Then I know I have someone who is willing to work with me to create a healthy relationship. Brant R. Burleson, professor of communications at Purdue University in Indiana, says, "The better friends you are, the more likely you'll face conflicts." So, yes, disagreements will arise, and there are ways to handle them so the relationship stays intact.

The first way to handle the disagreement is to actually handle it! Don't pretend it didn't happen. Don't pull away and give up on the relationship. (I'm not talking about a situation in which your friend had an affair with your husband. Clearly she is not your friend . . . and your core values are too different for a friendship to ever work. I'm talking about the little things we let add up until we explode . . . he is late to meet you for the one-hundredth time . . . she forgot to return the skirt she borrowed.) Pulling away won't mend the relationship, and it won't help your heart either.

We need to be willing to confront the issue that is seemingly dividing us . . . however big or small. Too many people are afraid of confrontation because they see it as a bad thing. *Confrontation* means "coming face to face." Confrontation is not attacking, being abusive, or voicing petty and nasty criticism. Confrontation is bringing to light an issue so that the friendship is restored and strengthened.

Sometimes you need to swallow your pride in order to mend a friendship.

Sometimes you need to swallow your pride in order to mend a friendship. Not that this is ever an easy thing to do . . . because most of the time I think I'm right and that it is obvious! Resolving conflict is always harder, if not impossible, when both parties are holding onto their egos . . . their pride. Warrior chicks will fight to keep the relationship healthy, and that means handling conflicts.

Recently one of my dearest friends said something that just about broke my heart. I was busy living life, speaking at conferences, traveling, and doing some media interviews. I called my friend in the midst of these busy few weeks, just to touch base . . . to connect with someone I loved. I was a little exhausted, and I always have to work harder to control my emotions when I am tired. We played phone tag for a few days, and then finally when we did speak she challenged me about what I was doing. Well, actually challenged is perhaps too strong of a word. But she definitely questioned my decision to do a few of the things I was doing. My feelings were hurt. It sounds a bit ridiculous as I write this . . . I think I made a mountain out of a molehill. She is a dear friend and certainly has the right to ask me questions about any decision I might be making, but I took it very personally. I could feel myself pulling away from her. Bad decision.

A few days later I summoned the courage to talk to her again . . . It wasn't easy. I was afraid of what she would think of me and the fact that my feelings were hurt. I was afraid bringing it up would make me look silly. I hate coming off as emotionally weak. However, I swallowed my pride and asked her what she meant when she had questioned me. She very simply explained, and cleared up the situation in one hug and one sentence. I breathed a sigh of relief. Looking back over my life, I wonder how many friendships I let slip away simply because I didn't have the courage to confront some uncomfortable feelings, or I let my pride get in the way of talking about those feelings. Sometimes it is easier to let things slide . . . but it is certainly not better. Warrior chicks have the courage to handle confrontation.

One time my friend Wendy said that she had something she needed to talk to me about. She then proceeded to tell me in a rather sheepish manner that she "hated my perfume." Now you might be thinking, *Why would she tell you something that really doesn't matter?* Well, we were about to take a fourteen-hour plane trip together . . . sitting side by side. And the fragrance I wore bothered her. There are a few responses to a comment like that. One is to say, "Too bad for you. This is my favorite perfume, and I am wearing it. You'll just have to sit at the other end of the plane from me." The other is to say, "No problem. I won't wear this one while I am around you." This may seem like a silly example, but I have seen friendships destroyed because of things just as silly! I truly appreciate the fact that Wendy was willing to tell me about the problem instead of just booking a seat at the other end of the plane and leaving me wondering what was going on . . . and maybe even getting my feelings hurt. And I am a big enough girl not to be offended that she doesn't like my perfume. I did not take it personally. The friendship is more valuable to me than my perfume.

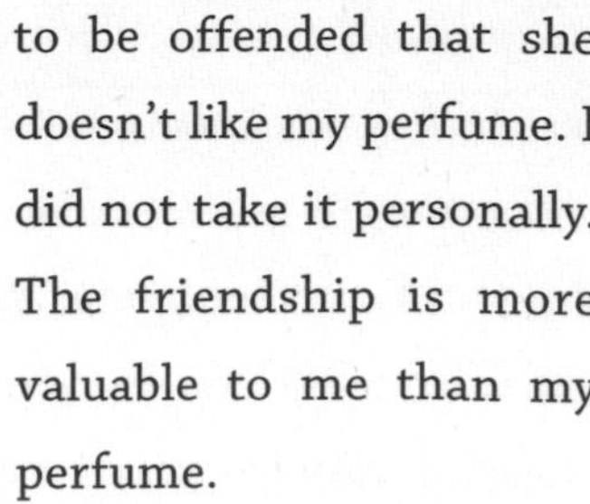

Sometimes conflict arises because each person has unspoken rules she expects every-one to obey.

Sometimes conflict arises because each person has unspoken rules she expects everyone to obey. Perhaps when you were growing up, your mother never really let you help in the kitchen . . . that was her domain. Now you are in a university, and you go to a friend's house for dinner. After dinner you continue to sit at the table and talk to your friend, who is in the kitchen cleaning up. It never occurs to you to offer to help because you were raised thinking that the kitchen belongs to the woman of the house. On the other hand, your friend is getting angrier the longer you continue to sit there because she was raised with the rule that everyone helps in the kitchen. If neither of you says anything, I guarantee you will never be invited to dinner again and never really know why. (When you come to my house, feel free to wash the dishes!)

I have a friend who has this rule that work-related questions can be asked only at work . . . not when we are out playing. She got angry with me the first time I did this, but I didn't know her rule—and she assumed everyone did.

This is also true in a marriage. Most of the time we enter a marriage with unspoken rules or notions of how we think marriage should be. I remember thinking that every man should know how to barbecue. Well, my husband didn't even know what charcoal was! And I thought the man was supposed to be able to fix anything that needed fixing . . . silly me! If it requires more than a hammer, my husband can't fix it. Of course, he thought all women could iron. Boy, was he in for a shock! So, if there are things that are important to you, make sure you are communicating them and not just assuming everyone knows.

In a conflict it helps to be able to see the situation from the other person's point of view. This is not easy, because most of us selfishly think our side of the story is the only true one! (Okay, maybe you're not like that, but I know I can be!) I have talked with countless numbers of people who have had friendships that have lasted decades. Most of them say that it has taken real tolerance in order to keep their friendships. They have also said that while handling conflict is important, the battles chosen are even more important. Good point. Choose the issues worthy of confrontation. Don't fight over every little thing. Realize that most disputes arise from a simple misunderstanding.

Jan Yager, author of *Friendshifts: The Power of Friendship and How It Shapes Our Lives,* recalls what happened after her father died, and a close friend didn't attend the funeral. "I felt hurt and disappointed," she says. Later Jan learned that her friend hadn't come to the service because she was still distraught over her own father's death. "My perspective changed entirely," explains Jan. "Rather than feeling slighted, I empathized with her."[3] Instead of immediately assuming the worst about a friend, perhaps we should give her a chance to explain.

For any issue to be resolved, we need a sit-down-and-face-the-issues conference—and usually more than one. Conflict is rarely solved accidentally. The solution must be approached deliberately and intentionally. Conflict is rarely solved on the run. Be prepared to fix the problem . . . not cast blame. Come ready to reconcile and resolve.

Certain ground rules have to be observed in conflict resolution. The United States and Russia have had treaties to ban certain weapons in the event of conflict, even though both countries were not in total agreement on certain issues. They just realized that nuclear weapons could destroy both nations. Perhaps it is the same in any relationship. We must eliminate verbal weapons that will do more harm than good. Watch for words such as *always* and *never* because usually they aren't true. And then, of course, remember what you tell your children: no hitting, no biting, no lying, no throwing things, no using bad words!

In any conflict, stay focused on the issue at hand. Don't bring out a list of all the things your spouse or friend has done over the years. Unrelated issues are off-limits. Don't blame or accuse. It's better to make the discussion about your personal feelings than it is to point an accusatory finger. Use statements such as "When ____ happens, I feel ___." Or "I need ___." Or "What would make me feel better is ___."

Using phrases that begin with "You should . . ." or "You need to . . ." or "You always . . ." will only escalate the conflict. Try to remain calm and logical. (I am aware that this is not always easy . . . but it is part of the price of being a grown-up!) You'll get better results if you can express yourself honestly and directly.

C'mon, Warrior Chick, if you have had a conflict, be willing to apologize . . . even if you were the one wronged. In the movie *Love Story*, a character commented that "love is never having to say you're sorry." I don't agree; I believe that love is about being the first one to say, "I'm sorry." Whether you were the one who was wronged or you were the one making the mistake, when someone apologizes either for making the mistake or for perhaps misunderstanding, the doors of communication are open. And then maybe the one who made the mistake can explain or admit the failure.

My hope is that I have given you some tools to help you negotiate the conflicts that come up in any relationship. Although there will be some people you might need to let go of, there will be more you should hang on to. So don't give up on the relationship just because of a minor conflict that has escalated into a big issue. Do your best to resolve it . . . even if it takes more than one attempt. As long as you are talking to each other, there is hope for restoration. Work hard to maintain the connection; relationships naturally go through ups and downs.

Lord, grant that I may seek
more to understand than to be understood.
—SAINT FRANCIS OF ASSISI

Okay, you God chicks. Let's be committed to being warriors!

- Rising with courage in the midst of tough times . . .
- courageously going after our dreams . . .
- courageously building relationships . . .
- courageously forgiving . . .
- courageously staying at the posts we have been assigned to . . .
- courageously being willing to lay down our lives . . . egos . . . rights . . .
- courageously facing the necessary battles . . . handling conflicts so that relationships remain strong.

A HERO IS SIMPLY
SOMEONE WHO
RISES ABOVE HER
OWN HUMAN
WEAKNESS,
FOR AN HOUR,
A DAY, A YEAR,
TO DO SOMETHING
STIRRING.

—Betty Deramus

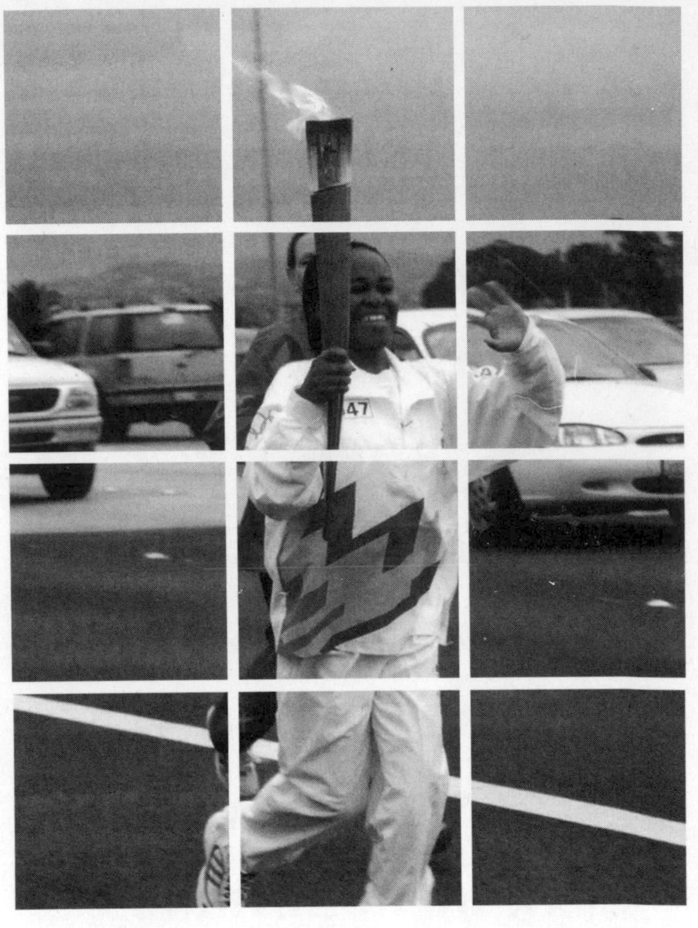

Champion Chick Mose carrying the Olympic torch.

Hang in there. Many of life's failures

are people who did not realize

how close they were

to success when

they gave up.

—Thomas Edison

CHAPTER FOUR

the champion chick . . .

She girds herself with spiritual, mental, and
physical strength for her God-given task,
and makes her arms strong and firm.

—OLD TESTAMENT, PROVERBS 31, VERSE 17

There are things you and I are supposed to do on the planet . . . and we need to have strength to do them! When I think of being strong, I think of muscles. I immediately think of going to the gym and lifting a thousand pounds! (Like I could do that?!) But we actually need much more than physical strength. We need spiritual and mental strength as well.

In order to be the force on the earth we are destined to be, we need to see ourselves as champions and adopt the characteristics of champions.

Okay, Champion Chick. What does it mean to be spiritually strong? I think it means that I hold on to what I know to be true and at the same time I am willing to grow in areas where I need to. It means that I don't waver in the knowledge that I am an irreplaceable, loved-beyond-measure daughter of the King. It means that I am more than capable of loving all different kinds of people, extending a hand where necessary. It means that I love my God more than my own life. It means that I know how to do the heaven exchange, exchanging my strength for God's, as my friend Darlene Zschech says. It means that my life produces good fruit continually. So how do I become this spiritually strong woman? I'm so glad you asked!

> *Most of my spiritual strength comes because I am connected to the house of God.*

Most of my spiritual strength comes because I am connected to the house of God. The psalmist told me that if I want to be flourishing in my old age (not that I am anywhere close to old age!!), if I want to be living a happy life (and who doesn't?), then I must be planted in a church. So many people who claim to love God are out on their own, disconnected from the rest of His body. We weren't created to flourish like that. The church is the very heartbeat of the Father, and we need to love it too. I am very aware that there are no perfect churches . . . because they are made up of people just like you and me . . . people on a journey. But if we are going to be strong and flourish, then we must plant ourselves in a local church.

I have seen too many people over the course of the years come to the church, begin to plant themselves, become offended about something, and so uproot themselves. Then they go to another imperfect church and begin the cycle again. The house of God should be the most dynamic, fun- and life-filled, and life-giving organization on the planet. I know that not all churches get this yet . . . and so I'm sorry if you have been to one that was boring (that should be a sin!), judgmental (Jesus never judged hurting people), and lethargic. But please keep trying, and find a church that you can plant yourself in, that you can commit to . . . because we need you to be strong and flourishing. We become a force on the earth when we are spiritually strong . . . not wavering with every new doctrine that comes along. Link arms with other women in the house of God, and take your place as the champion.

The champion is also mentally strong. She manages her reactions to stressful situations. Instead of reacting, she responds appropriately. This is where I have seen many women blow it. Life in the twenty-first century is huge, but God must think you can navigate it beautifully because He planned for you to be born and live in this time. If He had wanted you to be alive back in the days of *Braveheart* (just think of seeing men in those cute skirts!), I think He could have managed it. But He saved you for the twenty-first century! Yes, there is a lot going on . . . but you have the ability to mentally handle it!

Proverbs tells us that the God chick is capable and intelligent. Some of you are probably saying, "Lady, you didn't see my school grades!" Well, that was then and this is now! Now you have the chance to develop the mental strength you will need in order to become that force on the earth. Start wherever you are.

If you are going to be mentally strong, you must be willing to learn new things along the journey.

If you are going to be mentally strong, you must be willing to learn new things along the journey. If you are married, learn some new things about being a wife. Read a book on marriage. There are plenty out there. (Hey, I've even written one . . . mainly because I did so many dumb things in my own marriage, I thought I would share them and help someone else *not* do the same dumb things!) If you have children, I suggest you read a few parenting books. My children did not come with instructions, and I am very thankful there are great books available to help me. I have a teenage son . . . that is a new experience for me! I definitely have to be mentally strong, and right now I am reading a book on parenting teenage boys. I have listened to tapes and talked to other mothers who have sons who are now in their

twenties . . . I am really trying to get this. Can you tell!!?? I am committed to being a champion.

How about your career? Do you want to advance? Well then, I guarantee you, you will need to learn new things. Have you taken a class so you can be better at your job? Do you want a different job? Are you receiving training so that if you were to get it, you would be successful at it? If right now, you are working at Starbucks, but what you want to do is to be a marketing director for a Fortune 500 company, you must do a few things. Don't just ask God for that new job. Rather, put yourself in a position to receive it. Take a night class. Spend time with someone who has the kind of job you want. Read book after book.

As director of the women's ministry in our church, I had to learn a few things if I wanted it to really grow. I read books by other women who had great ministries, I listened to tapes, I watched videos, and I spent lots of time with some amazing women. I grew in my ability to lead. I had to increase my mental strength!

I need to be willing to think new thoughts. New thoughts will take me in a new direction. Old thoughts got me where I am—but I want to be continually growing, so I must be willing to open my mind to new thoughts. I don't want to get stuck in a routine or rut, and neither should you!

Champion chicks want to learn and grow. We want to be coached. A champion athlete is always asking her coach what she can do to improve. And when given direction, she doesn't become defensive. She adjusts whatever needs adjusting.

My husband loves to read—only he felt he read too slowly. He listened to a speed-reading course on cassette and began to put into practice some of what he had learned. One of the first things he had to do was to turn the book upside down and skim down the page. I guess because reading upside down was so hard, by the time he finally turned it right side up it was going to be easy! We were in an airport waiting for our plane as he began to practice this. I thought nothing of it until I saw people staring at him as he "read" the book upside down. I'm sure they were thinking, *Bless his heart, he is pretending he can read*. I started laughing (I laugh at lots of things!) and pointed out to Philip what was going on. He smiled and just continued with the exercise. I realized that it was more important for him to learn to speed-read than it was not to look silly.

So, sometimes, when you learn something new, you might not look very cool . . . but keep on going!

So, sometimes, when you learn something new, you might not look very cool . . . but keep on going! In order for my friend Kay to finish her race with strength, she had to go back to school and get an advanced degree. I'm sure it wasn't easy. She was probably the oldest in her class. She was also working full-time and had a family. You go, girl!! A true champion chick!

Being mentally strong also involves controlling our emotions. Too many of us are led through life by our emotions. And that will get us in trouble! Most of us will admit that having a high IQ would be helpful. However, Daniel Goleman, in his book *Emotional Intelligence,* challenges us to raise our EQs (emotional quotients). This is our ability to handle our emotions. There are thousands of very bright people on the planet who are not successful simply because they cannot control their emotions. When they are angry, they lash out; when they are sad, they fall apart. If you and I are going to be successful, we must learn to manage our emotions. We cannot do everything we *feel* like doing.

I love my husband, but there are times when love is not the most dominant emotion I feel. There are times when I am very angry or very sad or frustrated or lonely, and yet I don't let those emotions drive me out of my marriage. Love isn't just what I feel; it is what I do . . . oftentimes in spite of what I feel! There is something to be said for maintaining an even keel. I am not saying we should never express our emotions, but we should manage them. On a scale of one to ten, some of us react to a situation with a ten when a three might have been more appropriate. Sometimes the reason we explode is that we have let our emotions build up over time instead of handling situations as they arise.

There was an instance when I yelled at my son (I mean *yelled!!* . . . not good). Afterward I realized that while he had done something that made me angry, I was lashing out way beyond what was called for. And sure enough, I began to realize that other things had occurred that day . . . at work . . . with a friend . . . that I hadn't dealt with and so my unsuspecting son bore the brunt of more than his own misbehavior.

If we don't manage our emotions, then every time we feel like having ice cream, we have it. Not always a good thing! I do certain things not because I "feel" like doing them, but because I have made the decision to do them. A woman was feeling lonely (all of us have felt lonely at one time or another!). This feeling led her to a very inappropriate relationship from which she is still facing consequences. (A free tip . . . loneliness is something you must settle in your own heart . . . by pursuing the purpose you've been given by your Creator. Other people, though they may be distractions, are not cures for loneliness.) Some parents justify beating their children because the children made them "so angry." There will be consequences for not managing that anger. As a champion chick, I must be mentally strong. I must manage my emotions rather than let them manage me.

The champion chick is not only spiritually and mentally strong; she is also physically strong. I am not saying that we should all try to look like the female version of Arnold Schwarzenegger, but we should be committed to being as healthy and as strong as possible. I am also not saying we need to look like fashion models. A lot of their photos are airbrushed anyway. (I *know* . . . I walked down that path a while.) Life is full and busy today. We are pulled in various directions, and we must accomplish a lot on any given day. We must be strong if we are going to do what we must.

Whenever people ask me what I do for a living, I always pause and ask, "Which moment of the day are you talking about!?" I change jobs depending on the hour of the day. Sometimes I am a chef, sometimes I am a chauffeur, sometimes I am a pastor, sometimes I am an author, sometimes I am a motivational speaker, sometimes I am chief bottle washer, sometimes I am a cheerleader, and always I am a wife and mother . . . so . . . pick your moment! All those roles, along with a few others, are part of the destiny journey I am walking. And if I want not only to survive this journey, but also to be victorious in it, I must have physical strength.

It is hard to do what you are called to do on the planet if you are three hundred pounds overweight or thirty pounds underweight. If you have no muscle strength, how can you live the life you are created to live? Now, before you get mad at me . . . let me tell you why. Life is not going to get easier or any less busy. That is a fact. Not unless you totally withdraw from society and become a recluse. And as God chicks, we are supposed to be touching our world, not running from it! While all the roles I play in my life are demanding, I do not want to give up any of them. That means I have to manage them. And to do that, it will take strength—spiritual and mental as well as physical. I am not saying that we should be assuming roles that are not on destiny's path for us—be careful about that! But do get strong enough to handle what you should be handling.

I go to the gym and work out not because I am trying to win a bodybuilding contest (that will never happen!), but because

I am trying to build some muscles, keep my heart healthy, and keep the fat percentage of my body at a reasonable level. Because I have scoliosis, I often experience pain in my back. I have found, however, if I strengthen my abdominal muscles, my back feels much better and is stronger. Do you know how I strengthen my abs? By doing hundreds of different kinds of stomach crunches, leg lifts, and sit-ups. Is doing them ever fun? *No!!!* But I do them anyway because I know I need to be strong to accomplish all that I am put here to do. I can't afford to be lazy!

Also, by physically taking care of my body, I have found that I just feel better. And when I feel good, I make better decisions than when I am physically weak. When I am physically weak, I am more susceptible to stupid thoughts and more prone to illness.

When I feel good, I make better decisions than when I am physically weak.

So, come on, Champion Chick. Take care of your body . . . rest, exercise, and how about a massage every now and then!!? We have big lives to live, so let's get strong! I don't care if you are eighteen or seventy-eight, you can start now doing something to build strength. As God chicks, we have people to love and a world to touch. We can't be getting weak in the middle of the journey! Come on, you can do it!!

One woman who comes to our God chick meetings . . . an awesome gathering of hundreds of God's girls . . . was challenged when I gave this message. She was very overweight and had never recognized that she needed to be healthy, not just for herself, but for others, so that she could finish her race with strength. She finally understood the *why* of living a healthy life. She has since lost about eighty pounds and has more to go, but she has the idea now! I am to live my life in strength, not just for me, but for the many people that I am to touch. So, if you feel that you might be really overweight or just physically weak, get some help (there is plenty of help out there!) and begin the journey toward strength. We are counting on you! (Of course, talk to your doctor before starting a diet/exercise program.)

See yourself as an athlete who is constantly in training. Athletes watch what they eat. Champion racehorses are worth hundreds of thousands of dollars. Because they are so valuable, the trainers are very strict with their diet. The horses are given the best grain and the best supplements. Are you not more valuable than a horse?? Eat in a way that will give you a long and healthy life. Countless books on the market can give you direction. I'm just suggesting you start seeing yourself as worthy of a long life and do whatever you can to ensure that you get to live it!

When we see ourselves as champions, we will treat ourselves better. Cigarette smoking will not cause you to go to hell . . . although it might send you to heaven before you want to be there!! So I'm not sure that is a habit you want to keep very long!

We champion chicks should watch what is going into us . . . and I'm not just talking about food. I'm talking about what we ingest, not just through our mouths, but also through our eyes and our ears. We need to make sure that we are reading books that will help us along the journey. I love movies, but I don't just see every one out there. I try to be a bit careful with what I allow in.

One of my dearest friends is a woman named Joyce. She is an awesome black woman with whom I have had a friendship over the past ten years. I believe one of the mandates on my life is to bridge the gap racially . . . to demonstrate friendship that crosses all sorts of barriers. And Joyce and I have demonstrated a true friendship for many years. We respect and honor the gifts in each other. And we truly love each other.

Joyce is a woman of strong faith and conviction, not someone who could get deceived easily. I am saying that because there was a time when she was deceived. She made the choice to see a movie that brought confusion to her life. There is a very talented black filmmaker who also happens to be a bigot. Most of his movies are filled with racism. He is convinced that it is impossible for white people and black people to truly be friends. My friend Joyce went to see one of his movies and came out of there wondering if I was really her friend. She came out of the theater wondering if I could be trusted.

Thank goodness, she had the courage to at least call me and ask some questions. I yelled at her (well, just a little!) for even seeing a movie made by that guy, and then I reassured her that he is the liar. The truth is that I value her and what she brings to my life. What she allowed into her heart just about destroyed the job she and I have been trying to do in demonstrating racial reconciliation. I am telling her story (with her permission!) to illustrate the point that even if we think we are strong, what we allow into our hearts will affect us.

I love all kinds of music . . . but I am careful about what I listen to. I love spending time with people, but I am careful that I don't surround myself with gossip. What I allow in will affect me, so I am as careful as I can be. Guard yourself against the junk out there that would hinder you from running your race with excellence!

As champion chicks, we are to be strong. One of the definitions of *strength* is "durability." That means we can keep on going and going and going . . . just like that bunny on television! We were built to last!! Our God-given task is to finish out life amazingly . . . to finish the race we have been asked to run.

In 1992 at the Barcelona Olympics, Kerri Strug missed the all-around finals by 0.14 of a point, coming in fourth on the American gymnastics team. She tore her stomach muscles while training in 1993, and then in the summer of 1994, she fell from the uneven parallel bars and sprained her lower back. On July 23, 1996, for the first time in history, the U.S. Women's Gymnastics Olympic Team won gold. Kerri remembered nothing of what transpired in the air on her first vault of that Olympics, only the ominous sound and pain of her too-short landing. Her ankle gave way. The judges cast their vote in one minute. She had thirty seconds to decide what to do. Kerri remembered the pain of "missing the all-around finals at the

Barcelona Olympics and knew she didn't want to almost make it again." She didn't ask her coach the child's question: "Do I have to do this?" She asked the competitor's question: "Do we need this?" Everybody but the coaches and athletes knew the answer was no. Kerri did her second vault. She held the landing for the judges and then collapsed on the mat on all fours. As he carried her to receive her medal, her coach, Bela Karolyi, said of Kerri, "She has a heart of a tiger."[1] You go, Champion Chick Kerri!

The writer of the New Testament book of Hebrews told us that we are surrounded by a great cloud of witnesses. These are the men and women who have gone before us. I honor the women of past generations. Their lives and accomplishments have opened the door for me to be where I am on my journey. Now I take the responsibility for the baton they have placed in my hand. The baton has been passed to us . . . those who came before us did their part and did it well . . . now it is our turn to get it right. We are to run the race before us with strength and endurance.

We need the strength to start the race. All of us, from the moment of conception, were instilled by our Creator with everything we needed to live a magnificent life. Each of us was given the gifts necessary to live out the purpose she was given. Some of us have embraced our King and the destiny He gave us . . . we have begun our journey with Him . . . and some of us haven't started this yet.

If you are reading this and haven't begun your relationship with God, how about opening your heart to that now? It is only by knowing Him that you can understand your purpose. His hand is extended toward you—ready to lead you on the most amazing adventure. Go ahead—take His hand.

And on this journey called life, there are times when we need to start over . . . maybe we have fallen or made a mistake. We need to be able to pick ourselves up. As I mentioned in Chapter 3, I have a black belt in karate. One of the first things I learned in karate was how to fall and get back up. (That was not what I signed up for!! . . . nonetheless, that is what I spent the first months doing!) I learned to fall to the front and get back up; I learned to fall to the back and get back up. When I was learning this, I didn't really understand the purpose. I was just frustrated because I wanted to be learning the really cool stuff . . . and falling down did not qualify as cool.

However, months later, when I began to spar, I discovered the reason I learned how to fall and get up. Sometimes in sparring, I would be knocked to the ground. It was instinctive in me to just get back up . . . after all, I had been practicing the falling–getting up thing for months. So I didn't even have to think about it; I just got back up.

I have observed that some people on this journey through life may fall . . . but rather than getting back up, they lie there, asking why they fell. Or maybe they ask, "Why did God let this happen?" Or maybe they just lie there whining. Or maybe they give up. Come on, Champion, develop the strength to get up . . . to start over if you need to.

We have to be strong to last through the tough times. We must learn how to get over the hurdles that we encounter on our race. And we *will* face them. How are you going to handle the inevitable obstacles?

One obstacle that we all face on this race is offense. When someone offends you . . . are you going to let it knock you off course? Please don't let it. I have seen so many people get knocked off track because of an offense they are carrying in their hearts. In the race I am running, I will be running with certain people. If one of them does something that hurts my feelings, I have to quickly let it go; otherwise I will find myself withdrawing.

Too many people have stepped right into the trap of being offended. It is hard to run a race with your foot in a trap. It is always a shock to me when someone doesn't like me! But I have to be careful not to be offended. Recently a woman said some mean and critical things about me. Yes, her comments hurt me, but I couldn't dwell on the hurt for very long, or I would be knocking myself out of the race. I have to keep my focus on where I am going.

Offense is just one of the hurdles on this journey that I must get over. Some of us God chicks are stopped on our journeys because we are hung up on our past. Maybe we have run the race for a few years, and then we are stopped by who we used to be. We forget that as King's daughters we have a new identity. We all have a past, and the truth is it can be a hurdle that we must get over, but we honestly have to take a look at it. Your past experiences and your upbringing have helped to get you to where you are now and can propel you forward or hold you back. It's all in how you look at it.

Maybe you had some wonderful experiences in your past . . . named high-school valedictorian (I'm *so* impressed!), crowned Miss USA, surrounded by great friends, got a terrific education, raised by loving parents . . . you know, everything was wonderful. Well, if this is you, then perhaps the first time you encountered any difficulty, you were in shock. You might have been tempted to look back, wondering where the "good old days" went. If you are looking back longingly, then you can't run the race in front of you.

I heard a story about Tiger Woods, the champion golfer. A reporter asked him why he didn't keep his awards and trophies in his house. His answer was great. He said that he was focusing not on the accomplishments that represent his past but on his future.

On the other hand, perhaps your past was far from wonderful. Maybe your past was filled with pain, abuse, sin, sorrow, and disillusionment. Perhaps you carry the shame of your past, so you keep looking back and saying, "No wonder I can't succeed. Look at all that happened to me."

We have to acknowledge our pasts, good or bad, and then face forward, moving ahead. When we are driving in a car, the rearview mirror takes up a small percentage of our view. It is there so we can look back to see if we have run over anyone! But we don't spend our whole time looking in it, or else we wouldn't be very effective at moving forward. We would cause a lot of damage. It is the same with our lives. We need to acknowledge our pasts . . . whatever they were like . . . and then focus on where we are headed. Don't let the obstacle of your past keep you out of the race. You are the champion chick . . . keep on keepin' on!

Let me tell you the story of Wilma Rudolph, a little girl who was born in a shack in the backwoods of Tennessee. Believe it or not, she was the twentieth of twenty-two children! (Her mom must have been Superwoman!) She was born prematurely and was not expected to live. When she was four years old, she got really sick with both pneumonia and scarlet fever. These illnesses left her with a paralyzed left leg, and because of that she had to wear an iron leg brace.

But Wilma had one thing going for her. She had a mother who didn't understand "impossible." Her mother told her that she could do whatever she wanted to with her life. She just needed to have persistence and a lot of courage. (She is *really* starting to sound like Supermom now!)

When Wilma was nine years old, she took off the leg brace and shocked her doctors by taking the steps they never thought she would. She then developed her own unique stride. She liked walking so much, she thought she would try running—and then came up with the crazy idea of becoming the world's fastest runner.

When she was thirteen, she entered a race and came in last. During high school she entered every race, and came in last every time. People were embarrassed for her and begged her to quit. But, one day she came in next to last, until finally she won a race. From then on, she won every race she entered.

Wilma went to college and met a coach who believed in her. He saw her determined spirit, and recognized her talent. He trained her to go to the Olympics in Rome in 1960. (A far cry from the girl who was told she would never walk!) Her greatest competition in Rome was a runner from Germany named Jutta Heine. Up until then, Jutta had been undefeated. But in Rome, Wilma beat her in both the 100-meter dash and the 200-meter dash. She had won two Olympic gold medals!

But Wilma wasn't going to stop there. Her last event was the 400-meter relay, and once again she was to face Jutta. A relay race is won and lost in the baton exchange, and the first two runners on Wilma's team made perfect exchanges. However, as the third runner was handing the baton to Wilma, the runner dropped it.

Wilma saw that the German team, with Jutta in the lead, had taken off down the track. It seemed like it would be impossible for Wilma to catch up with her, but catch up she did. And then she passed Jutta to cross the finish line and win her third Olympic gold medal. She is the first woman to win three gold medals in the same Olympic games. What an amazing woman!

Maybe you don't have the limitations to overcome that Wilma did, but I would imagine that on your journey through life you have encountered some obstacles that screamed at you to quit. And maybe you didn't have the cheerleader mother telling you "You can do it." Well, allow me to be your cheerleader (I have my pom-poms out . . . scary picture I know) . . . YOU CAN DO IT! DON'T QUIT! OVERCOME THE OBSTACLES

ON THE PATH! WE ARE COUNTING ON YOU TO REACH THE FINISH LINE!

The richness of human experience would
lose something of rewarding joy
if there were not limitations to overcome.
—HELEN KELLER

As champion chicks, we need to have the strength to start the race . . . to start again if necessary . . . to overcome obstacles, and we need the strength to finish the race . . . to finish what we have started.

One of the weaknesses I noticed about myself was that I didn't always finish the projects I started. I am a great starter! It's just my finishing that needs work! Because I saw myself as weak in this area, it affected my self-confidence. I knew I needed a plan. I knew I needed to start something and then actually finish it. And it needed to be something significant . . . you know . . . something other than finishing a double-scoop cone!

At that time in my life, I was taking my son, Jordan, to karate class. (I have told you about the fear I felt as I was testing for my black belt . . . now let me tell you why I even started taking karate in the beginning.) As I watched the classes, I began to think, *I can do this*. Plus, I noticed that at every level a student passed, a new color of belt was given, all the way to the black belt. It was like a prize, and I like prizes!

So I signed up for karate. Perhaps it wasn't the easiest goal for me to reach, but that was what I did. I started as a white belt, and at every class I attended, I looked at the black belt on the wall and said, "You're mine!" The first day of class I showed up in my new white uniform and stiff white belt. I was so excited because I had seen the movie *Karate Kid* and I wanted to learn to do the amazing kick that was demonstrated at the end of the movie. I just knew it wouldn't be long before I wowed my family and friends with my amazing ability. Well . . . we didn't learn that amazing kick the first day or even the fortieth day! What a bummer! For months we learned how to fall. *Boring!!* I definitely wanted to quit, which had been my pattern for years.

As soon as a project got a little mundane or slightly boring, I would quit, feeling justified (because why should I have to put up with boring??), and look for something more exciting. Here's a little tip for free . . . sometimes life, marriage, and work are boring or just routine. Because we are grown-ups, our decisions during those times actually say a lot about our character. Previously the decisions I made during the boring part of projects revealed that I was a quitter. And I was determined to change that! So, there I was again, at a boring part of a goal. But that time I hung in there. I didn't quit . . . I kept the goal of the black belt in front of me.

Hang in there . . . don't quit . . . there is probably a reason for the boring part of the journey you are on. And take heart . . . it doesn't stay boring forever!

A few years into the karate challenge, my son decided that he wanted to devote most of his time to basketball, so he no longer wanted to study karate. Great . . . my karate goal became an inconvenience. It wasn't easy to figure out what to do with the rest of the family while I continued to take classes. I almost quit at that point. Another tip for free . . . reaching goals is never convenient.

Three years into the challenge it became really physically difficult. The actual karate moves I was required to learn were tough. The forms (a series of intricate movements) I had to memorize were complicated. I was wondering if I hadn't chosen too hard a goal for myself . . . plus I ended up with more bruises than I wanted!! Karate is a contact sport, and that was becoming more and more evident!

Four-and-a-half years later, I passed my black belt test. Yippeeee!!! Were there times when it had been boring? Yes! Were there times when I wanted to quit? Yes! Were there times when it was inconvenient? Yes! Were there times when it seemed too difficult? Yes! Just the fact that it *was* a difficult goal to finish made it even more valuable to me. Getting my black belt did things for my self-esteem that nothing else had done up to that point. I had started something and finished it! You can too. Pick something, anything. Find a goal, and begin the process of reaching it, overcoming all of the obstacles on the way . . . boredom, inconvenience, difficulties . . . and others. When you finally get there, you will feel amazing!

Usually I have found that we don't feel like quitting until the pain gets to be horrible. It's just like childbirth. We breathe right through the first few contractions. We are feeling like super-birthers! However, during the phase called transition, when the pain is at its most intense, we wonder why we ever started this! And if we could quit, we just might! But a lot of times, the intense pain we feel is a sign that victory may be close. On this journey, you will encounter times of difficulty and pain . . . but keep on going, you champion chick!

Champion chicks persevere. One definition of *persevere* is "to remain under without breaking." It's like resistance training. The reason my muscles become stronger and bigger when I work out is that the weights I am lifting provide resistance. I become a stronger person when I persevere. A definition of *perseverance* is "the ability to continue a course of action in spite of difficulty."

We can actually help each other persevere. My friend Shanelle ran the Los Angeles Marathon. I was definitely impressed. She said that around the nineteenth-mile mark, it became very difficult and she was ready to stop. (I would have been ready to stop around mile two!) What kept her going was the encouragement of the spectators. They yelled things like, "You can do it!" "Keep on going!" "You're doing great!" As she heard the cheers, she got another spurt of energy, which carried her over the finish line.

Champion chicks persevere.

Let's not quit until we have crossed the finish line. There is a story of a marathon runner from Tanzania who represented his country in the 1968 Mexico City Olympics. He entered the stadium to run his final lap one hour after the winner had been announced. He came in bloodied, hurt, and bandaged. Obviously there had been an accident somewhere along the way. A reporter asked, "Why didn't you just quit when you realized you had no chance to win?" The runner replied, "My country did not send me to start the race, but to finish it."

I have been sent to the planet not just to start the race, but also to finish it and finish strong. My Creator doesn't get glory in what I start; He gets glory in what I finish.

My Creator doesn't get glory in what I start; He gets glory in what I finish.

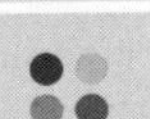

A major problem is that some of us have trouble sticking with something . . . no matter what. We can get scattered and unfocused going from one thing to the next . . . one marriage to the next . . . one job to the next . . . one friend to the next . . . one dream to the next . . . one town to the next . . . one church to the next.

No one else can run in your lane. In the sprint races of track and field, each runner must stay in her own lane. In one summer Olympics, a runner was disqualified from the race because of two false starts. And the interesting thing was, the camera that was positioned in his lane still recorded. It just recorded an empty lane. No one else could run in his lane.

You and I must be those champion chicks who become strong . . . in spirit, mind, and body. We must be the champions who overcome obstacles along the journey. We must persevere and not only start the race, but also finish it. Because if we don't, then the purposes for which we were sent here might not be realized. And there is a generation coming up behind us that needs us to finish our part of this race.

In a relay race, if the runner just stopped, ran out of strength, or got distracted by another runner before the baton pass . . . the team would lose. We have to finish our leg of this race so that those to whom we pass the baton can start strong and not have to recover ground. If we can get this generation of women to truly understand that they are princesses, warriors, and champions . . . and then live their lives as if they accept those roles . . . the next generation can move even farther ahead with confidence.

As a champion, I must train to improve my ability at the baton exchange. I am continually taking and passing off a baton. There are two groups I am in constant contact with, the people I am handing off to and the people I am receiving from. What I learn, I should be continually passing to a younger woman. And my hand should be extended to an older one, ready to receive the baton she puts in my hand.

The purpose of the relay race is to keep taking the baton farther. In the torch relay that opens the Olympics, the focus is on taking the torch farther. Our focus is on taking the message we've been asked to take even farther. The focus is not necessarily on us, although the goal won't be accomplished if we drop the torch . . . the baton.

There are some amazing women who have come before me . . . who ran their race and handed the baton to me and women of my generation. Now, I am running this race not for me, but for my children and my children's children. The baton will not be dropped on my watch!

We cannot tell what may happen to us in the strange medley of life. But we can decide what happens in us, how we take it, what we do with it—and that is what really counts in the end.

—Joseph Fort Newton

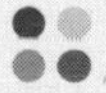

wherever you are,

it is your friends

who make your world . . .

—William James

CHAPTER FIVE

the friend chick . . .

Without friends, no one would choose to live, though he had all other goods.

—ARISTOTLE

In the not too distant past, I was having some challenges (nice word!) with my husband. He is a wonderful man . . . I just couldn't see it on this particular day. My feelings were hurt, and I was frustrated (anyone ever been there?). So what did I do? I called my friend and told her my woes. She listened and made all the appropriate comments. She let me go on and on and on. She is a good enough friend not to let me throw a pity party for too long or husband-bash indefinitely. And eventually she helped me find my way out of this discouraging place where I had found myself. Thank God for my friend.

In an earlier chapter I told you of my experience in a castle in Wales. It was truly awesome! There I was, staring at one of the most magnificent castles I have ever seen. (Keep in mind, I'm an American, and to me, any castle is amazing!) The view was awe-inspiring, almost bringing tears to my eyes. When I walked inside, I was touched by the history of the place . . . wondering about the women who had lived there. As I stood just looking and being amazed, the most wonderful thing happened . . . I grabbed the hand of my friend standing next to me and knew that she, too, was experiencing all the same emotions. Having someone to share the adventure with made all the difference in the world. Thank God for my friend.

Another time tears were streaming down my face as I realized that my son had a physical condition that might require hours of doctors' visits and years of medication (unless we received a miracle . . . which would be great!). Like most parents, I hated the thought that my child would have to face any difficulty. As I cried and reached deep inside for strength, I hugged my friend and knew that she was willing to help and be an encouragement along the journey. Thank God for my friend.

I was bent over double, laughing so hard that tears came to my eyes one day as I was shopping (one of life's great joys!) in an exclusive area of Sydney with my friend. We were trying on very silly outfits in an area of town filled with the very sophisticated. It was not a moment any man would have found funny.

But we laughed and laughed until our stomachs ached. Oh, the joy of shared laughter! Thank God for my friend.

Organization is one of life's little challenges for me. I can come up with all sorts of great ideas for a women's seminar, meeting, or conference, which will include different speakers, multimedia presentations, props . . . but actually carrying through with all the steps necessary to accomplish the goal is at times beyond me. My friend patiently waits while I express all of my enthusiasm and passion for the event and then quietly asks, "I suppose you want me to put it all together?" "Um . . . yeah . . . please," I reply. Thank God for my friend.

There is nothing more exciting for me than to stand on a stage and teach women how to live successful, joyous lives and to look in their faces and know they are getting it. Looking out at the women who are on life's journey with me, determined to finish the course set in front of them, is one of my favorite things. They make my life rewarding and full. Thank God for my friends.

And you know the really cool thing? Each one of these examples is a different woman. How great to have so many different women contributing to my life. I treasure these women.

We lead very busy lives, and sometimes in our busyness, the first thing to go is the time we spend with our friends. We have jobs, families, and activities that all pull at us, and oftentimes friendships are put on the back burner. I would like to suggest that the friendships you build are crucial to your happiness and your success in this life.

You and I were not created to go through life alone. We are part of an awesome company of women around the planet. If we are going to fulfill what we were created to fulfill, we will do it by connecting and staying connected to the people who join us on the journey. Each of us must be the friend chick. We were not created to solve all life's problems on our own. We do not have all the answers. We need each other!

As virtuous women, we are part of an awesome company of women around the planet.

Maybe you have overcome tremendous obstacles on your journey through life. There are women who need to know how you did it. Perhaps you have single-handedly raised your children to responsible adults (a miracle for any of us!). Well, I guarantee you there is a woman in your circle of influence who needs to know what you did and how you did it.

Perhaps you have overcome tremendous marital obstacles, managed to stay married and still love that man! Some of us need to know what you know. Build a relationship with a young woman who could use some of your wisdom. Or you may have lived through tremendous abuse, and you have found the path of healing . . . well, there is a woman somewhere who is still trapped in it and needs your help. Maybe you have overcome serious debt and could give someone a few pointers on how to get out of it. Your past can help someone else have a future . . . but only if you are willing to build relationships. There is also someone out there who can give you hope in what you are going through . . . but only if you reach out.

I read an interview in *O, the Oprah Magazine* (actually it was more like we got to eavesdrop on a conversation) between Oprah Winfrey and Jane Fonda. Jane made the observation that she had lived the first two acts of her life and now at sixty-two was beginning act three. She wanted this last act of her life to mean something . . . she wanted it to help make sense of the first two. She has learned some valuable lessons in her life, which she included in this interview.[1] I loved reading her comments because I started thinking, *This is what it's supposed to be like!* . . . the older woman passing on the lessons of her life to the younger one. I am a woman just in act two; I need the older woman to share what she knows and has learned. Friendships aren't just for you; they are to help those around you. In the interview, Jane also commented that at the end of her life, she wanted to be surrounded by people who love her and whom she loves . . . and she realized she had some work to do in order for that to be a reality. At least she's starting now.

Friendships are vital. They can be an avenue of hope when there is none. They can be a place of inspiration when you are depleted of all energy. They can provide laughter just when you need a smile, and a prayer when you need a miracle. C'mon, girls. We need each other. Let's get good at building friendships!!

So just how do we go about building friendships that will not only affect our own lives but also impact a world that needs to see love in action? How do we become the friend chicks we were destined to be? So glad you asked!!

One way to build friendships is to show acceptance in spite of differences that may exist between us.

When I walk on the beach to watch the sunset, I do not call out,
"A little more orange over to the right, please," or
"Would you mind giving us less purple in the back?"
No, I enjoy the always-different sunsets as they are.
We do well to do the same with people we love.
—CARL ROGERS[2]

"Make a decision . . . just make one! And please make it before the end of this century!" It was beginning to be painful to shop with my friend. It took her forever to make up her mind, and she doubted my comment that the blue skirt made her rear end look big. I admit that the blue skirt wasn't really all that bad; I just wanted to get out of this store and on to the next one! And then she had the audacity to tell the store clerk that she would think about it and that we would be back. Not a chance!! We were finished with this store. There was nothing to think about . . . the red or the blue . . . how hard was that??? Why couldn't she be like me?

If my friend told me one more time that she needed me to itemize the budget, being careful that the numbers stayed in the correct columns, I was going to scream!! And then she proceeded to tell me that there was a computer class that could help me learn to do budgets using charts and graphs, which, of course, she loved. Fat chance!! Why couldn't she be like me?

Never mind my bloodshot eyes and the dark circles under them. I was not tired! . . . and I proceeded to tell that to my very bossy friend who was trying to get me to rest. Couldn't she see there was still fun to be had at this leadership training conference and I didn't want to miss it? We got into a very intense discussion (fight) as she attempted to instruct me in the ways to take care of myself, what I should eat, what kind of exercise I needed, and how much sleep I should be getting. What is she . . . my mother?? Why couldn't she chill out and be more like me?

Hundreds of years ago, Hippocrates discovered that there were basically four different personality types. And that all of us are some sort of combination of those four types. When he came up with the types, it was not to put people in a box, but to understand why certain people reacted the way they did. He gave us tools to better understand each other and to learn to communicate with different people in a much more effective way.

One personality type is the *sanguine*. They are the "party-waiting-to-happen," "confetti-in-a-bottle" people! They are lively and energetic, and they can talk to anyone at any time. These people are very easy to spot when walking into a room because everything about them is open and moving—mouth, hands, and eyes! They use big gestures to make a point, and they laugh frequently and loudly. They make friends easily and love to be with people. These people prevent dull moments, and if you don't know any, you should definitely hire some for your next party! They will keep it moving! Because of their energy and zest for life, they are great in front of people, leading meetings or motivating volunteers. When they send you an e-mail, it will often include all CAPITALIZED words and lots of exclamation marks!!!!!! (Of course, they have to actually remember your address! ☺) On the other hand, sanguine people may suffer from foot-in-mouth disease (because they are talking so much of the time!) and try to dominate conversations. They don't tend to be very organized, and they can forget things they are supposed to remember. Generally they are great starters, but finishing projects can be a real challenge! And they can be motivated by feelings rather than reality.

Another personality type is the *melancholy.* These people are the deep thinkers in our society . . . they even tend to be genius prone! They can solve problems most of us don't even want to spell! These are the very creative and artistic people. They actually *use* daily planners! (The sanguine generally buy planners because they look good!) For the most part the people with the melancholy type of personality are very neat and tidy, and they like to live in an orderly and organized environment. Not finishing what they start is not an option; of course, the job will be finished! They make friends cautiously, unlike the sanguine who jumps into relationships with both feet, not sure exactly where they will land! Melancholy personality types are faithful and devoted friends, being moved to tears with compassion.

Most have a very dry sense of humor that can keep you laughing at any time. When they send you an e-mail, it is grammatically correct, with no misspelled words—they actually use spell check! (They probably invented it!) They can, however, be very negative, finding fault in many situations as if it were buried treasure! They can get perturbed if a house isn't kept in just the way they think it should be and angry if someone is late to an appointment with them. They tend to be pessimistic, often seeing the glass half empty. And because they like perfection and life certainly isn't perfect, they can become depressed when life and other people don't measure up to what they expect or want.

The *choleric* is another personality type. These people are born leaders . . . the other personality types learn to be leaders . . . these are born wanting to take over! They are goal setters and have goals for everything. Unlike the sanguine, these people won't get distracted trying to get from point A to point B. If you don't have an opinion, they will tell you what yours is! And if it takes you too long to finish your sentence, they will finish it for you!! In an emergency it is great to have cholerics around because they know what to do or will fake it until someone who really does comes along! They are energetic and can accomplish many tasks at once . . . doing whatever it takes. They really like e-mail because the job gets done quicker and they don't have to chitchat over a lot of trivial stuff. They are not easily discouraged, and they move quickly to action. Like the sanguine, because of their confidence, they are great in front of people.

They can, however, try to drive people rather than lead them. And they can leave out the fun in their quest to get the job done. They can step on people and those people's feelings on their journey to get the job done . . . ouch!

The *phlegmatic* is another personality type. And this one can be difficult to spot because they are a little chameleonlike—becoming whatever is necessary in any given situation. They are not extremely anything. Generally they are easygoing and relaxed, peaceful and agreeable. These people are great listeners and compassionate toward people and their problems. They can, however, be unenthusiastic and indecisive. It takes them quite a while to make up their minds about most things, and generally they prefer the status quo. It might take a stick of dynamite to get them to move or to try something new! They prefer to wear the most casual thing the situation will allow. I heard Florence Littauer teaching one time, and she said that phlegmatics can be a bit lazy . . . if standing becomes too tiring, they will lean; if leaning becomes exhausting, they will sit . . . until eventually they are practically lying down!

I love learning and studying about the different personality types, trying to figure out which one I am (actually that is not that hard . . . I am the loud party-waiting-to-happen sanguine!), but the higher purpose is to better understand others. The goal is to understand them and value them, not view them as wrong! There is no wrong personality!!

Realize that someone with a different personality from yours will handle situations differently from the way you would handle them. That does not make her wrong! Understanding this concept has helped me be accepting of my different friends, and it has actually helped around our office. While each personality type can do many kinds of jobs, generally there is a job where each will thrive. For a job that requires extreme attention to detail, generally we found that someone with the melancholy personality is better suited. If we need someone to counsel people through grief, usually a phlegmatic is best. If the job requires constant interaction with people, such as customer service, a sanguine will thrive. A choleric is great for jobs requiring someone with drive and initiative. For an office to be fully effective, people of all personalities are needed. For my life to be richer, for me to fulfill my destiny, I need to build relationships with people who have different personalities.

So instead of thinking . . . *That girl is just too picky and detailed for me!* . . . learn to value her for her organizational skills.

Instead of thinking . . . *That girl is too hyper and too scattered!* . . . make the choice to value her for her energy and spontaneity.

Instead of thinking . . . *That girl is too pushy, always in a hurry to tell me what to do!* . . . be grateful that she's in your life because you probably go more places and see more things.

Instead of thinking . . . *That girl is a slug and hardly says two words!* . . . be grateful for her peaceful presence in a chaotic world.

Too often we look only for people who are just like us to be friends. How many great friendships are we missing out on? Jeremy Taylor said that a wise man seeks friends with qualities he himself lacks.

> *No one person can possibly combine all*
> *the elements supposed to make up what everyone*
> *means by friendship.*
>
> —Francis Marion Crawford

As a friend, I try to value not only the friendship, but also the person. There is nothing more wonderful than spending time with someone who truly values you . . . someone you *know* likes you. I want my friends to feel valued, and one of the ways I can do that is to love who they *are* . . . not who I wish they were! Love the differences between you and your friends . . . don't just tolerate them, but love them! It is not always easy because sometimes the differences seem insurmountable!

The friendships we build should be an ever-increasing circle. We need to keep our hearts and minds open and accepting of friends who are different from us.

There are plenty of differences between people that some have let get in the way of friendship. Let's not be like that!

Find value in making friends with someone of a different generation. We can learn so much from those younger and older than we are. My marriage survived a very rocky patch because I took the time to develop a relationship with an older woman

> *Love the differences between you and your friends . . . don't just tolerate them, but love them!*

who could help me through it. (She wouldn't let me kill him . . . which, of course, I was considering! . . . and she reminded me of some of the reasons I loved him . . . I had conveniently forgotten those!) My first child also survived babyhood (he's happy about this!) because I spent time with experienced mothers. I enjoyed spending time with other first-time mothers like myself, but I truly got help from those just a little older. Find a woman who has climbed the mountain you want to scale, and let her open your eyes to new possibilities.

Also find a younger woman . . . someone who is perhaps struggling with a giant you have already killed. She needs you, and there are things you can learn from her . . . maybe some new, fun way to dress or wear your hair! My friend Anjanette is fourteen years younger than I am. She keeps me in touch with new thoughts, styles, and ideas. And because I believe one of my most important jobs on the planet is to encourage, inspire, train, and teach the generation of girls right behind me, she keeps me on my toes. I can't just tell her the best way to live her life; I have to model it. No pressure there!! We have been invaluable to each other.

Make friends with someone of a different culture. The world

is a big place, but we can make it smaller if, within our own communities, we are pulling down the racial barrier. We can make a difference in our own lives and in the world if we go beyond our comfort zone and truly build relationships with people who look and think differently.

Recently I was asked to be a guest on a daytime talk show in the U.S. Initially the producer wanted me to discuss how women of different cultures could be friends. I was very happy to do this because not only do I think it is possible for women of different cultures to be friends, but I also think it is crucial. I have started small groups within our church with women of very different backgrounds, and we managed to move from acquaintances to true friends . . . so I know it is possible and I wanted to share my experience.

A few days before I was to do the taping, someone from the show called me and said there were going to be a few changes. Instead of a show demonstrating that women of different cultures could be friends, they wanted me to come on and basically fight with someone who was different in a demonstration of why we *couldn't* be friends. Needless to say, I declined the offer. I realize they are after high ratings, and a fight does generate them. I was just not willing to be a part of it. I believe one of the reasons I have been put on the planet is to demonstrate healthy relationships and teach others how to have them. I truly think the world is ready for some help and not just looking for silly—and sometimes destructive—entertainment on TV.

Build a friendship with someone who has different interests from yours. Of course, it is important to share some interests. And naturally we are drawn to those with whom we share dreams and goals. That's great! I'm just suggesting that we open our circle to include someone who likes different things from what we do. Maybe you have never been a sports enthusiast, and the activity is far from your favorite thing. (You are still grumbling over the fact that you were always picked last for the softball team!!) But your life will be richer if you spend time with your friend who loves sports . . . Even if you never end up being Ms. Jock, at least your friend will feel important because you took the time to do something with her that didn't come easily to you. Maybe you like country music (don't be shocked . . . there are a few of us!!) and your friend is into jazz. How about going with her to a jazz concert? Perhaps your music tastes will expand, but if not, you will have made her feel important because you supported her in something. What if you hate coffee? So? Go with her to Starbucks anyway! You can get something else to drink there. The time together is priceless.

God chicks today come in all shapes, shades, and sizes. They come in all styles. Some wear panty hose. Some don't. Some are into sports. Some aren't. Some like rap music. Some don't. Some have *lots* of ear piercings. Some don't. Some have multiple colors in their hair. Some don't. Some are married. Some aren't. Some have high-powered careers. Some don't. Some have tattoos. Some gag at just the thought. Some speak English. Some don't. Some can dance. Some can't. Some have children. Some don't. Don't let the fact that your sister is different from you cause you to reject her.

C'mon, girls . . . instead of trying to mold our friends in our own image, let's love them just the way they are! Let's accept certain limits. We can't be angry with someone who is six feet two because we want her to be five feet eight, but sometimes we communicate that about hidden things. While we should all be growing and becoming stronger in certain areas of our lives, certain things in people are not going to change. Let's accept people for who they are. The truth is, they will only be better versions of themselves and not whole different people! As the American writer Allan Gurganus said, "If you are a person's friend, you don't harp on things you know are past their ever changing."

Build friendships with those of different personalities, age groups, and backgrounds.

Build friendships with those of different personalities, age groups, and backgrounds. Will it be easy? No! It is never easy getting out of our comfort zone! It is never easy to prefer someone else! But I do know our lives will be the richer for it!!

Another way that we build friendships is to remain loyal. *Loyalty*, according to Mr. Webster, means "devoted to, to stand by, to fulfill promises," and it means "to forsake any ambition that compromises the relationship." What I have found is that many people are loyal as long as it's convenient, until something better comes along, or until someone comes along who can do more for them, so then they ditch an old friend for a new one.

It is not so much our friends'
help that helps us as the confident
knowledge that they will help us.
—EPICURUS

As children, we're friends with the kid who has the best toys or the best backyard (or in my case . . . the cutest brother!). If some kid comes along who has more, a car, a better stereo, a more handsome brother . . . whatever . . . we start hanging out with her.

When you're loyal, you're committed through the difficult times. I used to think that every relationship was 50-50. But that is so wrong! In every relationship, there are times when one person is doing most of the giving. Sometimes it's 70-30, sometimes it's 40-60, and sometimes one is so weak or in a tough spot that it's 100-0! It can be exhausting to listen to a friend who is going through a tough, emotional time. (Not for you phlegmatics, of course!!) But as loyal friends, we are supportive as they work through the pain. After all, there will come a time when we will need the same support! If we are loyal, we stick by them in the hard times.

> One could not but be moved by the story of the soldier who asked his officer if he might go out into the "No Man's Land" between the trenches in World War I to bring in one of his comrades who lay grievously wounded. "You can go," said the officer, "but it's not worth it. Your friend is probably killed, and you will throw your own life away." But the man went. Somehow he managed to get to his friend, hoist him onto his shoulder, and bring him back to the trenches. The two of them tumbled in together and lay in the trench bottom. The officer looked very tenderly on the would-be-rescuer, and then he said, "I told you it wouldn't be worth it. Your friend is dead and you are mortally wounded." "It was worth it, though, sir," he said. "How do you mean, 'worth it'? I tell you your friend is dead." "Yes sir," the boy answered, "but it was worth it, because when I got to him he was still alive, and he said to me, 'Jim, I knew you'd come.'"[3]

There was a time when I was so frustrated in my marriage that I was ready to throw in the towel (or throw it at him!!). During that time, I know I was not a very giving friend. I was very self-focused. However, I did have a friend, Diane, who stood by my side. She gave me some great bits of advice, but more than that, I felt loved by her. She met me for coffee, lunch, a good cry . . . whatever. She let me, time and time again, pour my heart out. At that time in our friendship, I was giving about 0 percent to her. I can see now where it could have been very frustrating to her! But she stood by me in my tough time, and her loyalty to me and to my marriage did pull me to safety.

I have noticed that oftentimes it is harder for someone to be loyal when things are going great in a friend's life. Recently I was in a room full of women. (Some men came in, took one look, and quickly backed out! . . . too much estrogen I guess!) One of my friends in the room asked me what was going on with me, and when I filled her in on the latest in my life (some upcoming television stuff in an arena that was new for all of us), she was thrilled. She got so excited for me.

Another woman there didn't really want to hear what was going on. She asked no questions and just turned away. Perhaps she wasn't interested, and that's okay (we do all have our own lives we're living), but because she is my friend, I wish she had shown *some* interest in my life, even though it might have been difficult for her. A lot of the wonderful things going on in my life are the result of finding the purpose God put me on the earth to accomplish and just living it out. I am not more special than anyone else . . . and I know that.

It is, however, fairly easy to rejoice with your friend when something good happens to her that you aren't particularly interested in happening to you. When I took my black belt test, I invited some friends to watch the test and quietly cheer me on as I sweated my way to victory! They could get excited about this achievement of mine because none of them wanted anything to do with high kicks, punching bags, or being knocked on their rear ends! They could freely get excited for me. Or maybe you know someone who is having her tenth child. (AAAGH!!) It is easy to rejoice with her because you don't want anything to do with ten children!! But what if something happens to your friend that you wish would happen to you? Can you rejoice with her then?

What if you're single and your friend who has been single (but not nearly as long as you have!) is getting married. Can you be happy, truly happy, for her? Or are you feeling things like this:

- "Hey, *I'm* the one who went to Jenny Craig and lost all this weight!!"
- "What's the deal? *I'm* the one who had my eyeliner and lips tattooed for around-the-clock beauty!"
- "*I'm* the one who's spent hours learning about football!"
- "*I* even took classes on relinquishing the remote control!"
- "What's the deal with this? I should be getting married next! *I'm* the one who's been a bridesmaid seventeen times!"

Why aren't we able to rejoice with someone in the good times? Perhaps it is jealousy or envy . . . and these are not emotions to be proud of! If you do find yourself feeling jealous, it should be an indication to you of a slight sense of insecurity and perhaps frustration in that you aren't aware of your purpose and destiny. You can work on that! (See Chapter 1: "The Just B U Chick"!) Seeing someone else accomplishing her goals should be an encouragement to you that it can be done. Knowing that someone else is fulfilling her purpose doesn't take away from your fulfilling yours. Each of us was put on the planet to accomplish her own unique destiny. My destiny is linked to other people. I truly believe that when our friends are walking in theirs, it should thrill us because as our friends fulfill their destiny, we will too.

Can you rejoice with your friend, even during those times when it might be tough to do so? Can you be happy for your friend as she discovers she is pregnant with her third child and you have been trying to conceive for ten years? The desire for a child and the desire for a meaningful relationship are God-given, so I can understand how it would be a challenge to be happy for your friend or even be around her as she celebrates these momentous occasions. And on the flip side, if you are the one pregnant or getting married, can you be sensitive and patient while your friend works it out? Danielle Schlass in *Working Mother* magazine gives advice to a pregnant woman with a friend who has been trying to conceive:

> While your pregnancy is good news to you, it may have been devastating to your friend. You won't be able to hide your burgeoning belly or the new addition to the family from your friend, but a lasting friendship is possible if you broach the subject in a very sensitive manner, says Linda Applegarth, EdD, director of psychological services at the Center for Reproductive Medicine and Infertility at Cornell University Medical Center in New York City. Applegarth suggests that if

> you have accidentally blurted out your impending joy to your neighbor (which is understandable), try apologizing for the insensitive way it may have come across. Explain to her that you understand that this is a difficult situation for her, but you value the friendship and you'll be there for her if she needs you. Let any discussion about the baby be on your friend's terms. Let her know that while you're happy to answer any questions about your pregnancy, if she doesn't want to talk about it, that's fine too. Let her be the one to bring it up.[4]

If we would only be willing for a moment to see life from the friend's perspective, then we could be sensitive when necessary and be able to rejoice when it is important for the friend that we do. Taking our eyes off ourselves is a significant step in displaying loyalty.

In Los Angeles, where I live, quite a few of my friends are involved in the entertainment industry. There are times when more than one of them will be auditioning for the same part. My challenge to them is to be happy for their friend and not withdraw with jealousy if she gets the part. I'm not saying this is easy for most of us; I just know that to be loyal friends, we must stick by them in the good and bad times.

Friendships take time to build . . . think Crock-Pot, not microwave! Sarah Orne Jewett said that the growth of true friendship may be a lifelong affair. And the truth is that we are a part of the instant generation . . . the drive-through crowd. Generally if something takes longer than ten minutes, we won't wait. We are the "I want it and I want it *now*" people! I am the same way. I don't like waiting for anything. But friendship is different . . . it grows over time. And not just the passing of time itself, but the time we invest in the friendship.

> *There should be a word for that middle ground between acquaintance and friendship, where all is possibility, awaiting the test of time.*
>
> —ANONYMOUS

Understanding the way friendship works is a little like looking at a puzzle. There are many pieces in a puzzle, and each is a different size or shape. And there are many different people in our lives, each taking up a different-size piece in our hearts. Most people start out as acquaintances. And our puzzles are filled with these pieces. These are the people we know a little about . . . the waitress at a favorite café, the student in the chemistry class, the other soccer mom, the girl who works downstairs, or the hairdresser.

Other pieces in our puzzles, which are a little bigger, are the people we work with on a regular basis or see at some regular activity, such as a sports team, a book club, or a church. We are not really intimate with them, but we might know a lot about them.

The next biggest pieces in our puzzles are friends . . . those with whom we are working out the issues of friendship that I am writing about in this chapter.

Last, there are the largest and probably the fewest pieces in the puzzles . . . our intimate friendships . . . the sisters of our hearts. Not everyone will become an intimate friend, and that's okay, although I think it is definitely important to have more than one! In fact, I'm teaching my daughter that it's good to have more than one best friend. One person can't and shouldn't be everything to you. That's way too much pressure to put on someone! (Your husband should be one of your intimate friends, although not the only one or you will drive him nuts!) How does someone go from being an acquaintance to being an intimate friend?

The first step, I believe, has to be some form of agreement. This doesn't mean you agree about everything, but you acknowledge the same basic core values. You've heard the expression "birds of a feather flock together." The reason they flock together is that they are headed the same direction. Your intimate friends will also be headed the same way. Perhaps your friendship begins with an agreement about commitment to family or your faith; perhaps your agreement comes in that you and your friends are very committed to careers or to a common global cause. What is deeply important to you? It will also be important to the people who are your intimate friends. These agreements may start out as unstated, but the more you spend time with someone, the more the values become evident. Eventually you will talk about them, discovering if you are truly in agreement with your friend.

Obviously we respect the different characteristics of our friends, such as taste and style—learning to find the joy and humor in them—but our intimate friends have the same or very similar core values. They may not be expressed the same way, but the heart of each issue is similar. For example, if honoring and preserving your marriage is a core value of yours, it would be hard to be a friend with someone who regularly cheats on her husband.

Not only should there be some form of agreement in the core values, but in order for a piece in the friendship puzzle to grow from acquaintance to friend or intimate friend, there must be an investment of time. The passing of time alone does not grow a friend; it's what we do with that time. Taking time out of an already busy schedule (I'm sure you've got one of those too!) to spend with a friend may require extra planning, but I have learned that my life is much richer when I do.

At a seminar about friendships I taught a few of the principles that I have mentioned in this book. Afterward a woman came up to me and said, "I know friendships are important. I just couldn't manage to fit them into my very busy life. Thanks for giving me some ideas about how to make my friendships stronger. I will now take the time." And actually she was just one of a few women who realized how important friendships are in their already overloaded lives. Women just like you. Women with busy lives . . . jobs . . . careers . . . husbands . . . children.

C'mon, give your friends a piece of your time. Quite a few of my intimate friends live in other states, even other countries. But I don't let that be an excuse . . . some people are supposed to be forever friends, so I do whatever it takes to maintain the friendship. I have spent a number of hours with my friends Chris and Dianne at airport lounges as they lay over at Los Angeles airport. Getting to the airport is always a nightmare . . . but the joy of connecting with my friends is worth it. I have taken short flights to another city to catch my friend Shanelle as she jets around the globe. I have a husband, two children, and a job that require my time and my heart, so I don't get many of these trips, but I take them whenever I can. No, it is never convenient. Friendship rarely is. If I am given the choice between a new couch and a trip to see my friend Bobbie, I'll take the trip every time. My relationships with my friends are eternal; the couch will need reupholstering in a few years!

It should be much easier to find the time to build relationships with the women in your own city or neighborhood. If you have small children, meet at the park or some brave woman's home! If the children are older and in school, meet with your friends for coffee . . . you just need to connect every now and then. If you are working, take one evening once in a while to be with the girls. It can be done. To build the relationship from acquaintance to friend, time needs to be invested. And there are lots of creative ways to do that.

My friend Lisa gets together with some women every other month in a book club. These women find it a great excuse to have a glass of wine and talk. It is a terrific way for women to get together, because not only do they have a different book to discuss each time, but more than likely those conversations will lead to discussions about everything else that is going on in their lives. They get a chance to talk about work and family in a low-pressure, easy environment.

In generations gone by, women of different ages connected around a quilt they were creating, at a barn raising, at the birthing of a baby, or just over a cup of coffee in a home. But with so many women in the workforce, we must get creative and not give up on making the connection. Many times a friendship falls through the cracks just because we haven't given it any time. Go ahead . . . water that friendship and see if it grows!

There are also some simple ways to give your friends some time. I love cards. I love shopping for cards. I love buying cards to give to my friends. I love receiving cards. Whenever I get on a plane, I take the first few moments to jot down a thought and put it on a card to mail to a friend. How hard is that?! When I receive a note or card from my friend, it touches my heart deeply, not just for what the card says, but also for the fact that for a few moments in her day, she was thinking of me. I would imagine it does the same for her, so I take the time to let her know how important she is to me. A phone call, fax, or e-mail can be a quick way to connect with a friend and build the friendship that will last. It really isn't that hard. Sometimes I call my friend Bobbie, and I really have nothing earth-shattering to say. (She lives in Sydney, I'm in Los Angeles . . . at the prices of phone calls, I should be saying something earth-shattering!) It's just a way to stay connected. Sometimes we'll start to say good-bye, and one of us will think of about five more things to say! And often I'll call a friend, get an answering machine (doesn't anybody stay at home anymore??), and leave a quick "Hello, I was thinking of you" message. I love e-mail (especially when I can't find any postage stamps!). It doesn't have to be a long note; a quick sentence will do. Any of these methods will work. Just take the time to connect with your friend.

For a relationship to grow into an intimate friendship, it takes both of you wanting it to. If you see the possibility of a friendship growing, invest in it. If your want-to-be-friend sees and invests, too, you have struck gold! Don't, however, spend too much time wanting to be friends with someone who doesn't want to be friends with you. There are plenty of women in the world who do want to be your friend! Realize that for this time in history, she may just be an acquaintance or casual friend, and that's okay. (Here's a tip for free . . . this concept applies to our relationships with men too. When the man you are dating doesn't want a relationship anymore, let it end graciously. Show respect for yourself and him; don't force, manipulate, or pressure.) It is a drag to feel pressured into being someone's friend, so don't do that. There are other women waiting to be your friend!

Many times as children we are possessive of our friends . . . not really wanting them to have other friends. We feel abandoned and hurt if they develop a new friendship. We can't be like that. Really. We should rejoice! You want your friend to have lots of friends contributing to her life. You cannot be everything to her . . . it would wear you out. And your friend can't be everything to you. Each of us has strengths, and the different people you allow into your heart will bring different strengths to your life. I can't say this enough . . . keep your heart open.

A tragic event occurred at Harvard University in 1995. At the end of the spring semester, Sinedu Tadesse, a third-year undergraduate student from Addis Ababa, took a hunting knife and stabbed her roommate Trang Phuong Ho repeatedly. Thao Nguyen, a guest who had spent the night, and who was a best friend of Trang's, was also stabbed. After Sinedu murdered the friend, who in her mind had abandoned her, Sinedu hanged herself. Sinedu had felt that, in Trang, she had found her one true friend, and so felt abandoned when she heard that Trang would no longer be rooming with her the following year. Instead of welcoming Trang's friend Thao into their circle, she became jealous and possessive with disastrous results. Now, this is certainly an extreme situation, and most of us would never murder someone. But perhaps what we do is pull away when a friend makes another friend. Let's not do that. Surely our hearts are big enough for one more person.

I love the little song that I used to sing at summer camps: "Make new friends, but keep the old, one is silver and the other is gold." Those of you with daughters, encourage them in this principle . . . it will help them immensely as they grow. And the best way for them to get it is to see you model an open, easy, accepting friendship. Possessiveness, a desire for exclusivity, and a view of other people as a threat to the friendship are all signs of inappropriate dependence.

each friend represents
a world in us,
a world possibly not born
until they arrive,
and it is only by this meeting
that a new world is born

—Anaïs Nin, The Diary of Anaïs Nin Vol. II

Wherever you are, it is your friends
who make your world.
—William James

The pieces in your puzzle will change shapes. Some will grow smaller, and some will become bigger. You need to let people come and go. Always keep your heart open for friends. You could meet one of the best friends you will ever have next week! The borders of your puzzle should always be expanding, meaning your life should continue to enlarge with people. I'm sure, because you are human, you have been hurt and betrayed a time or two by friends. Yes, it is very painful. But please don't allow the hurt to become bitterness and then cause you to close your heart to people! Friends, who *all* start out just as people you meet, are truly one of heaven's greatest gifts to you!

The last how-to I will leave you with in becoming a friend chick is to challenge you to be willing to be intimate.

Oh, the comfort, the inexpressible comfort of feeling safe
with a person, having neither to weigh thoughts nor measure
words, but pouring them all right out, just as they are,
chaff and grain together; certain that a faithful
hand will take and sift them, keep what is worth keeping,
and then with the breath of kindness throw the rest away.
—Dinah Maria Mulock Craik[5]

These times are going to take real friends. Jack Nicholson said in the movie *A Few Good Men*, "You can't handle the truth!"

(Actually I went to see the movie for the Tom Cruise factor . . . the Nicholson statement was a bonus!) We need friends today who can handle the truth. According to a *USA Today* "Snapshot," 43 percent of the women polled said they would rather share a worry or fear with a friend than with a spouse, a relative, or a physician. So the truth is that we would *like* to share the secrets of our hearts, our dreams, and our fears with a friend, but for one reason or another, we aren't always willing.

I remember an instance in our church that involved a young couple. They had been coming to the church for a while, always remaining on the outskirts. One day they came to me as their pastor and described a crisis they were in. I felt bad for them and certainly offered what help I could. But what made me sad was that they had no one with whom they had been intimate, no real friend to stand by them and help them through this situation. Life can be tough. (You've probably figured that out by now!) We need friends who truly *know* us so that the tough times we face are bearable.

An actress admitted that her inability to truly be intimate has been at the core of her marriage breakups. And she knows it keeps her friends, even her daughter, at a distance. At least now she is realizing that in order for her life to finish strong, she must develop the ability to be intimate. So must you and I. Yes, it might be scary . . . but a life without intimacy is really no life at all.

Terri Apter and Ruthellen Josselson in their book *Best Friends* agree that "things happen to us, and we do things we need to talk about—and yet we don't want everyone to know. We share our feeling of danger and insecurity, or we confess to behavior that we feel is bad or humiliating. We can tell a friend because she'll be on our side: We count on her to see things from our point of view, to support us, even if she may disagree with what we've done."[6] If a friend doesn't see things from your point of view, or support you, then you must deal with the feelings of betrayal that will follow. I'll talk about this later on.

Most of us have a dream in our hearts. We need a friend we can share that dream with, so that when it seems as if it is not coming to pass, she can continue to offer encouragement. Without the encouragement of my friends, there are many things I would have given up on. But they couldn't have encouraged me if I hadn't opened my heart and shared its secrets . . . dreams as well as fears. Sometimes we try so hard to be independent. We really weren't created to live independently; we are to live interdependently . . . linked to each other. And this happens as we are willing to be intimate. I like this saying: "A friend is someone who knows the song in your heart and can sing it back to you when you have forgotten the words." She can sing it back only if you have shown her your heart (and actually, with my voice, it would be better for the song to be in my heart and someone else to sing it!)

To build a friendship and to keep one from dying requires intimacy. Let's get real! We need to get over our fear of betrayal so that we can open our hearts. One thing that keeps us from opening our hearts to others is the fear of being hurt or let down. If you are alive, you have probably been betrayed. I haven't met anyone who hasn't been.

To keep betrayal to a minimum, however, there are some guidelines in being intimate. You can't just share a deepest fear, secret, or dream with someone who hasn't proved that she can handle it. Don't share the story of your life with someone you have just met! When you share something with someone without really knowing how she'll handle it, you risk betrayal, which is certainly painful. When you wait until you feel you know and trust someone, you still might be betrayed, but at least you have been wiser with whom you share your secrets. You trust someone based not on her potential, but on the results in her life.

I've heard people say, "Well, she didn't mean to do all that hurtful stuff to you; she has a good heart." No, if someone has a good heart, then she doesn't consistently hurt you. You can't get sentimental and continue to open your heart to that girl you've "known since kindergarten" if she continues to betray you. If she gossips about others, she will gossip about you.

To test whether someone can handle intimacy, share something small with her. If she keeps that to herself, then you can share something bigger. Let someone prove herself faithful with a small portion of your heart before you give her a bigger portion. (It's just like a job. You wouldn't promote anyone to a better position if she hadn't been successful at the first one.)

Susan L. Taylor wrote in her book *In the Spirit:* "Not everyone is healthy enough to have a front row seat in our lives."[7] The more you look for respect, the more you grow in your own character, the more you look for love and truth in the world around you, the easier it will become to decide who gets to sit in the front row and who is relegated to the balcony of your life. The bottom line is, yes, you need to be intimate with friends, and there are some guidelines to follow in choosing with whom you are intimate.

Some simple gestures create an atmosphere of intimacy such as eating together, working on a project together, giving gifts and words—either written or spoken. Have a meal with your friend every now and then (especially those meals where you don't count calories!). There is an atmosphere of intimacy that can happen when you laugh and talk over a meal. Many of my relationships have grown as my friends and I have worked together on a project . . . whether it is a women's meeting, something at my children's school, or some kind of home-decorating thing (which I am pathetic at, by the way!). The time spent together, the late nights, the endless cups of coffee—all provide an atmosphere of intimacy.

There are ways to provide opportunities for intimacy, but true intimacy involves communication. Sooner or later you have to talk and really share with a friend if you want the friendship to be meaningful. Terri Apter and Ruthellen Josselson say it like this: "Talk is the currency of friendship. The route to sympathy, understanding and connection is through talk."[8] If this sounds uncomfortable to you, then begin by asking questions of your friend, such as:

- "What is the most exciting thing that has happened to you so far?"

- "What is your biggest fear?"
- "What is the dumbest thing you have ever done?"
- "What do you think you are really good at?"
- "What is your most embarrassing moment?" (This should provide a lot of laughs!)
- "What do you love most about your husband (or boyfriend)?"
- "What is something you want to accomplish before you die?"

These are just ideas. But asking questions conveys to your friend that you are interested, and as she answers, she opens her heart to you. A true treasure.

While intimacy is crucial for any friendship to truly develop, timing is also essential. Be conscious of the day your friend has had, the season she is in. If you just got an amazing promotion and you call your friend, only to find out she was fired, waiting a day or two to share your news might be best. You want to give her a chance to rejoice with you, and she very well might . . . just give her a day to recover. What you can do is listen to her. A verse in the New Testament tells us to "rejoice with those who rejoice, and weep with those who weep" (Rom. 12:15). I also learned this lesson with my husband. If I have some great news (maybe I'm pregnant or I won the lottery or something!), then I wait until he is in a place to rejoice with me (not when he is in a meeting!).

I also think it is important that you tell your friend how

much you value the friendship . . . that you don't take it for granted. Don't wait until your friend's funeral to say the nice things you think about her. Don't wait until she is dead to eulogize! Tell her now! Not too long ago I was at a funeral and heard friends and family alike saying some really wonderful things about the person who was lying in the casket. I remember wishing that she could hear the terrific things being said about her. I hope they told her these things before she died. Please don't wait until someone's funeral to say all the good things you have been thinking. It will do her no good then!

Recently I received a letter from a friend who is close in heart, but in reality lives thousands of miles away. She wrote words I will always treasure:

> Dear Holly,
>
> It was great to talk with you on the phone. Oh, how I miss the uniqueness of our friendship . . . being able to share ideas, exchange dreams, be grumpy, sad, silly, a slave to funky fashion . . . with you I can share times when I am feeling lost . . . you have held my hand through life . . . what a gift . . . I am grateful.

Sigh . . . how wonderful to have a friend who shares her feelings.

A few months ago, I was visiting my friend and saw a letter that I had written to her tacked to the wall in her kitchen. It was just a silly little note in which I expressed gratitude for our friendship. As I was looking at the note and smiling, she told me that a few teenage girls, who were friends of her sons, had been in the house and read the note. Their response was interesting. They had looked at her longingly and said they hoped one day they would have a friend who would write them a note like that.

We all crave deep friendships. We were born with a need for them. But they don't come just by wanting them. They come as we give the time, share the dreams of our hearts, and are willing to be intimate. I feel that one of my jobs is to model healthy friendships for those in the upcoming generation . . . and I take that job very seriously!

In fact, I am now training my daughter about this. (Another tip for free for you mothers out there. Your daughter learns how to connect and be intimate with her friends as she watches you . . . so what are you modeling? Just a question.) When my daughter, Paris, was seven, she told me how much she liked her friend Audrey. I asked her if she had told that to Audrey. She told me she hadn't and looked at me funny for asking. I suggested to her that the next time she talked to Audrey on the phone she should tell her that she's glad they're friends. It wasn't long before they were on the phone, and I heard my daughter tell her friend how glad she was for the friendship.

Tell your friend, in a note, a call, or face-to-face, how much you count on her friendship. Tell her the things you love about her. Tell her the dreams in your heart. Tell her what you are afraid of. Just tell her.

It's better to have
a friend than
go it alone.
Share the work;
share the wealth.
And if one falls down,
the other helps.
But if there is
no one to help, tough!
By yourself you're
unprotected;
with a friend you can
face the worst.

—Old Testament, Ecclesiastes 4,
verses 9–12 (The Message)

Laugh 'till you can't laugh . . .

and then laugh some more!

CHAPTER SIX

the party chick . . .

It is a happy talent to know how to play.

—Ralph Waldo Emerson

One morning at seven o'clock, I was in the kitchen doing the breakfast show. (Those of you with school-age children know what I mean!) Sometimes I think God should have given women about four hands . . . or at least have given us the option! I was making breakfast for Philip, Jordan, and Paris (pouring milk into bowls of cereal . . . chef that I am!) and making coffee at the same time. We women can do multiple tasks like these . . . or rather I thought we could! I was pouring boiling water into a filter of coffee grounds when the cup tilted over. Boiling water and very hot coffee grounds poured onto my arm. *Ouch!!!!! I* immediately stuck my arm into a sink of very cold water and continued to pour juice into glasses . . . after all, I had to get breakfast finished. (What a woman!!) My arm began to feel better . . . mainly because the ice water had numbed it!

My husband came into the kitchen, took one look at my arm in the sink, and said that we had better call the doctor. He commented on the fact that my skin was peeling off . . . and that he was seeing layers of my skin he didn't think he was supposed to (men . . . so squeamish!!). Nonetheless, he called the doctor and described the burn. Because the burn actually went all around my arm, I was told I needed to go to the emergency room so that my arm wouldn't swell up and fall off (or something like that!).

So off to the emergency room we went. I was in excruciating pain because the numbness of the ice had worn off. At the hospital, my arm was bandaged, and I was given a shot of Demerol for the pain. I have never had Demerol . . . the strongest painkiller I've had is Tylenol. But when the nurse described the woozy, floaty feeling I would have with the Demerol, I told her to give me that shot! The pain was so intense, I wanted the woozy feeling!!! I was looking forward to feeling floaty and pain-free!!

However, about five minutes after I was given the shot, rather than the spaced-out feeling I was hoping for . . . my blood pressure had dropped to 50/20 and was continuing to drop . . . and my heart was headed for arrest. I remember lying on the gurney, hearing my husband making the comment that

I didn't look too good. (Thanks, honey!) Then I heard the nurses yelling down the hall that they needed help in here. (I guess my condition was serious.)

In the midst of this commotion, I could feel my body shutting down . . . but my mind was still functioning . . . well, as much as it does at any time! I started to laugh in my head, *This is an* ER *episode . . . that's what it is . . . a woman goes in for burn treatment and ends up with a heart attack!* Well, thank God for technology. The medical personnel did whatever they needed to do to bring me back. A few hours later, I was sitting up and feeling better (although the arm still hurt!!! Are you feeling sorry for me??).

After my near-death experience, I am very glad to be alive! My suggestion is that we don't wait for an experience like that to cause us to love life. Jesus told His followers that He came to bring life . . . not death or destruction . . . but life. And the word that He used for "life" is the Greek word *zoe*. This word implies more than the breathe-in, breathe-out kind of life (although I am grateful to be breathing in and breathing out!). This word means abundant, overflowing, rich, and plentiful life!!

So, come on, you party chicks, we should be living life with passion. Life is for loving!!! We should be celebrating the life we have been given . . . not just trudging through the days, but really living them!

One of the ways we can enjoy life is to celebrate the moments we are given. We have different abilities and different talents. (Some of you can actually sing on key!) We come from different backgrounds and families. However, there is one

What are you doing with your now moment?

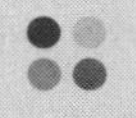

thing that we are all given that is exactly the same. Each of us is given twenty-four hours in a day, seven days in a week, and fifty-two weeks in a year. We are given the moment called *now.* And this moment will not come again. We are to live each moment. Time then becomes our responsibility. We are given now only once. What are you doing with your *now* moment?

> *The aim of life is to live, and to*
> *live means to be aware, joyously, drunkenly,*
> *serenely, divinely aware.*
> —Henry Miller

I should be living out every moment of my day fulfilling the purpose for which I have been created. Destiny isn't a destination, but a journey . . . it is living every moment the way I was created to . . . so every day of my life I am living out my destiny. This does not mean that I run around like a crazy person all day. No. It means that I make every moment count. My purpose on the earth includes being a wife, mother, teacher, author, and friend. So, whether I am cooking dinner (it happens occasionally!), helping my kids with homework (algebra is my specialty!), writing, studying, praying, talking (among other things . . . ☺) with my husband . . . I am living out my destiny and making the moments count.

Sometimes we mess up our *now* moments by not living in them. A number of us women work outside the home. What I find in talking to women is that rather than being in the moment at work, we are wrestling with feelings of guilt, or at the least, we are wondering if we did everything we could for our kids that morning. Or maybe we are concerned about all the stuff we have to do around the house. So we are not living in our *now* moment at work. We are not present. And then, when we get home, oftentimes we are wondering if we finished everything we were supposed to do at work. So we are not fully present at home either.

Maybe while we are sitting at church or a seminar we are wondering where we will go to lunch and with whom we should go. Maybe while we are having a conversation with someone, we stop listening and begin thinking about the weekend. So once again we are not living in our *now* moment. These moments become wasted ones simply because we aren't fully present in them. Party chicks live in the moment they have been given. We have got to quit wishing we were somewhere else!

From the time we were young (okay, some of us still are!) we put off enjoying the *now* moment. When we were fifteen, we could hardly wait to turn sixteen so that we could drive. Then we would be really happy once we graduated from high school. No, we'd be happy once we got accepted into the college of our choice. Then we'd be happy once we graduated from college. No, we'd be happy once we got that job we wanted. No, we'd really start living once we got married. It would be great once we had kids. We'd be happy once the kids were in school. No, we'd be happy once we got divorced. We'd be happy when we changed jobs. We'd be happy once we retired . . . and the list of waiting to enjoy the moments goes on and on. Looking forward to something is great, but not at the expense of enjoying the *now* moment. Live the moment you are in to its fullest!

You can't kill time without injuring eternity.

—HENRY DAVID THOREAU

We have a responsibility to live each moment fulfilling the mission we have been given on earth . . . because if we don't, we not only hurt ourselves, but we also injure eternity.

God has put me on the earth to fulfill a unique and wonderful destiny, and I should be doing all I can to fulfill it and not getting distracted by other things. The truth is, I am not going to be knocked off the course of my life by "bad" things. I am not tempted by the wares of the drug dealer on the corner or by Mr. Muscle Man walking by flexing his biceps. These things might still tempt some of you, and your battle will be to resist them as you focus on fulfilling your purpose on the earth.

No, I am not really tempted by the "bad"; however, I can be tempted to veer off course by opportunities that look "good." One time I was asked to be president of the Parent/Teacher Fellowship (PTF) at the school where my children go. It was an honor to be asked, and I like to be in charge of things (☺), so I thought that it would be perfect!

I went home to discuss this with my husband, who then loudly posed the question, "Are you nuts??!" After I assured him that I wasn't, he more calmly challenged me about my purpose in life and asked me if being the president of the PTF was a part of it. Knowing that being president would require time, he asked me which hours of the day I could devote to the job. All of these were good questions . . . okay, well, not the one about me being nuts! And I realized that, while being fun, the job of PTF president was not on the path of the race I am running. Was it a bad thing? No, of course not! It was a good thing . . . just not the best for me. It was someone else's best. You and I need to be investing the moments we've been given, doing the things that propel us along the path of destiny . . . and not getting distracted by the bad or the good.

As party chicks, we need to learn to value *now,* and we need to celebrate the victories . . . even the small ones. Sometimes we are so focused on the next goal that we don't take time to rejoice over the one we just reached. I'm sure many of you reading this book have had babies. You tell me, but isn't it true that as soon as the baby is out of the mother's body, the focus is on the baby?

I say, "Hold on just a moment!! The attention can go to junior in a minute, but right now, I'm celebrating the fact that I just pushed something the size of a watermelon out of an opening the size of a walnut! I am an amazing woman!! Let's party!!" Take a moment and celebrate that you did it! Did you just finish a class? Party!! Did you just lose those thirty pounds? Well, celebrate!! (You might want to leave out the pizza, though!) Is your son finally potty trained? Have a celebration . . . even if it is just a few moments. Did you finally find the perfect pair of shoes for that outfit? *Yippeeee!!!* Birthdays, anniversaries, and graduations are obvious times to party . . . but don't overlook celebrating the smaller victories!

What will set us apart from most of the world is being able to rejoice even in the midst of challenges.

So, yes, I find any excuse to celebrate and take it! However, what will set us apart from most of the world is being able to rejoice even in the midst of challenges. The apostle James instructed us that if we want to be perfect (and who doesn't??), then we will learn to find joy in the midst of difficulties. Most of us can smile when things are going our way, but I would like to paint the picture of the party chick as that amazing girl who can smile when it seems nothing is going her way. That's power.

My friend Bunny Wilson is a great party chick. Not long ago I heard her speak at a seminar, and as she was walking to the stage, I noticed that her hand was shaking. As soon as she reached the podium, she commented on her shaking hand. She said that she had gone to see a doctor and had tests run. The conclusion was that she had a generational tremor. Her mother had it, and her older brother had gotten it as he approached the age of fifty. Bunny, now fifty, had a shaking hand. Although she wants a miracle healing . . . who wouldn't? . . . she is smiling in the midst of this challenge.

She told the story of her conversation with her ten-year-old daughter, Gabrielle. They were trying to figure out what was good about a shaking hand. Her daughter commented on the fact that she would be an enthusiastic flag waver at a parade. Then she realized that her mother would be great at scratching backs . . . she could do it without moving her arm! And how about stirring a pot on the stove? She would be perfect at it!

I was in awe as I listened to my friend relate how she was looking for the good in the midst of her trial. She stands on platforms and speaks to thousands of women. I am sure she is not thrilled with the tremor, but somehow, some way, she is choosing to see the good.

You may be facing a challenge or trial. I don't know where it falls on a scale from one to ten. Maybe you are in the midst of utter devastation. I am sorry. If I were standing next to you, I would hug you and let you cry on my shoulder. Eventually, however, I would encourage you to search for the joy. Joy isn't some flighty, fluffy emotion. It is far more powerful than being happy. It is the steel that runs through your body. It is your strength.

If you are in a tough situation, why not have an "I'm looking for the joy" party? Sometimes we withdraw when we go through the tough stuff. I'm suggesting that you throw a party instead. Send out invitations! Say, "I'm going through the worst month of my life [I've gotten a doctor's report with scary news . . . I lost my job . . . whatever], and I would like you to come over and help me find my joy. You bring the ice cream." I'm not suggesting you act as if you are not having a hard time, nor am I suggesting that you pretend everything is all right. I am suggesting that in spite of the hard time you are going through, you should look for something good. And sometimes we need the help of others to find it.

One of my favorite Bible verses is 2 Corinthians 2:14, which says that "God leads us from place to place in one perpetual victory parade" (THE MESSAGE). I love this picture! Your Creator is leading you in a victory parade. He wants the best for you. Now, I am not so naive as to think that we go through life as if we were leaping from mountaintop to mountaintop to mountaintop to heaven. No, I know that there are valleys in between some of those mountains. But the fact that I am in a victory parade doesn't change!

"God leads us from place to place in one perpetual victory parade" (THE MESSAGE).

Even though I may walk through some valleys in my life, God will show me the way out if I let Him lead me. He is the God who makes beauty out of ashes. And there are some of us who have plenty of ashes to spread around! He can make something great out of the pain you are in or have gone through.

Mothers Against Drunk Drivers (MADD) was started by Candace Lightner. Her thirteen-year-old daughter, Cari, was killed by a drunk driver. Two days before that fatal accident, the offender had been released on bail for a hit-and-run drunk driving crash. He already had two drunk-driving convictions. At the time of Cari's death, the drunk-driving offender was carrying a valid California driver's license. I am sure Candace was enraged at the injustice of a repeat drunk-driving offender having a driver's license. I am . . . and it's not my daughter that he killed.

I don't know Candace. Maybe one day I will have that honor. But what I do know is that she allowed the party chick to surface. She could have let the anger cause her to withdraw. She could have become a bitter old woman. Instead, she let God make something beautiful out of the ashes of her pain. Along with some other mothers, she formed an organization that has had a tremendous impact on the drunk driving laws in our country. Somehow, some way, she let good come out of this horrible situation. *You go, girl!!*

Okay . . . so I like confetti . . . I like it a lot . . . and I will throw it at any opportunity! I think we have been given life to enjoy, and I am doing my best to make sure I do that!!

Party chicks approach life in an open way. I love the picture of the woman living life with her eyes open, her mouth open (!), and her heart open. There are a few definitions of *open*. One is . . . "accessible." The party chick is open. She is not hidden

Girls just want to have fun!

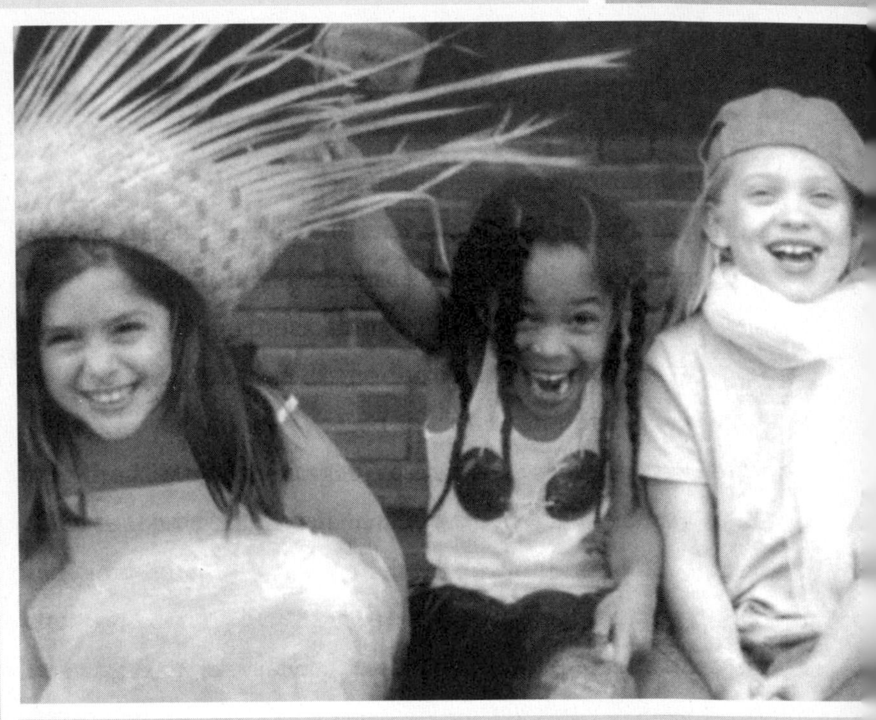

behind attitudes, fears, or ego. Another definition of *open* is . . . "a lack of pretense." Who you see is who you get. How very refreshing that is! She is not one way at work and another at church. She is the same person on Sunday that she was on Friday. Another definition of *open* is . . . "receptive to new ideas." She is the girl who is willing to grow and think new thoughts. She is expanding her brain! She is a learner.

The party chick keeps her eyes open. And they are open for a few reasons. We do need to open our eyes to the pain and suffering we see in the world—not just so that we'll cry and feel hopeless, but so that we can do something. Everyday situations come across our paths, and if we open our eyes, we can see we are being given chances to help. Jesus told a story about a man who went on a journey and was besieged by robbers who beat him mercilessly. He was cast to the side of the road and abandoned. Two other travelers came upon him and looked at him, but they did nothing. Another man came by and saw the man in his distress. The third man then bandaged up the injured man and took him to an inn to recover. One of the differences between the three men is that only one *saw* the hurt man. The others merely looked. Seeing always prompts some kind of action. So let's be the chicks who see . . . with a mind to then do.

Let's be the chicks who see . . . with a mind to then do.

Yes, our eyes need to be open so that we can bring some relief to the suffering that might come across our paths. However, equally important, our eyes need to be open to the wondrous things on the earth!

Here's a tale of two cities:

> A traveler nearing a great city asked a woman seated by the wayside, "What are the people like in the city?"
>
> "How were the people where you came from?"
>
> "A terrible lot," the traveler responded. "Mean, untrustworthy, detestable in all respects."
>
> "Ah," said the woman, "you will find them the same in the city ahead."
>
> Scarcely was the first traveler gone when another one stopped and also inquired about the people in the city before him. Again, the old woman asked about the people in the place the traveler had left.
>
> "They were fine people; honest, industrious and generous to a fault. I was sorry to leave," declared the second traveler.
>
> Responded the wise woman: "So you will find them in the city ahead."[1]

If you look for fault in someone, you will find it . . . it's not that hard. If you look for mistakes, you'll find them. If you look for where the world has gone wrong, you'll see it. If you look for the messes the youth generation has made, you'll find them.

But . . . how about if we look for wondrous things!?! How about if we look for the great things in each other? How about if we look for the amazing things on the earth? How about if we look at the energy and creativity of the youth generation?

One of U2's songs says that we should see that "it's a beautiful day," and we are not to let it get away from us.

All of us wake up every morning and get to make a choice about our attitudes. Some people have said to me, "You are too happy." No, I have the opportunity just as you do every day to choose, and I choose happy.

The apostle Paul challenged us to think on whatever things are true, whatever things are noble, whatever things are just, whatever things are pure, whatever things are lovely, and whatever things are praiseworthy (Phil. 4:8). I believe that what we think on and how we see life are interwoven.

> Finally, brethren, whatever things are true, whatever things are just, whatever things are pure, whatever things are lovely, whatever things are of good report, if there is any virtue and if there is anything praiseworthy—meditate on these things.
>
> The things which you learned and received and heard and saw in me, these do, and the God of peace will be with you. (Philippians, verses 8–9)

I am not a naive blonde cheerleader (well . . . not really!) who can't face reality. My husband, as cute as he is, is not perfect. I can look at all the things he doesn't do right, or I can focus on what he does that is wonderful. It is my choice. My son is sixteen, and there are times I don't relate at all to the way he thinks *and* I am ready to send him to boarding school in Antarctica! However, I make myself see the amazing qualities in him, and there are plenty. My daughter is very strong-willed and knows just what she wants. (Wonder where she gets that?!) I can let that drive me crazy or I can focus on the fact that she's a natural leader.

On a daily basis, choosing to see the glass half full, choosing to be optimistic, will help us not only see the possibilities, but also reach them.

If we want to be successful, we need to make optimism a part of our makeup, even though we are surrounded by negativity all day.

Most people choose the negative; honestly, it's easy to do. However, if we want to be successful, we need to make optimism a part of our makeup, even though we are surrounded by negativity all day. I have found that usually the best things for us are not necessarily the easiest. Going to McDonald's is certainly easy (and I have to admit that I do love the French fries!), but the food there is probably not the best steady diet for us.

A *U.S. News and World Report* cover story explained that "happiness can be learned by practicing it day in and day out.

Happiness comes when we take time to focus on the positive in our lives."[2] In addition, a recent book titled *Learned Optimism* notes that we can learn to have an optimistic outlook on life. It truly is up to us and not the circumstances.

Here's a story that delivers the ultimate optimistic statement. My friend Sarah Hummel is a young woman in her early twenties. She was recently married and then was diagnosed with Hodgkin's disease. She is a pretty amazing God chick. During her first hospital stay, she was known around the hospital for her upbeat personality and warm smile. Because of the chemotherapy, she lost her hair, but she always joked about being bald. She would say things like, "Hey, at least I don't have to worry if my hair looks good or not!" She made a point not to dwell on her sickness all the time. She worked hard at not getting overwhelmed by the journey of healing in front of her. She focused on what she had to deal with in the moment, rather than worrying about next week's chemotherapy. She said that it was easier to stay optimistic when she focused on the short term. She could be strong in the moment, but if she looked at the battle down the road she would be tempted to get overwhelmed.

There was always someone from the church at Sarah's house, not because they were feeling sorry for her, although I'm sure some were, but rather because Sarah's house was a fun place to be. And actually her husband said that they invited people over who laughed and who could see the humor even in the dark times.

Even at her weakest, she focused on the needs of others . . . always asking what she could do to help them with their hurt. One of the greatest examples of choosing your attitude came after one of her many bouts of chemotherapy. She was sick, as many people get after chemotherapy, and was throwing up. Now, I don't know about you, but I hate throwing up. I am not a pretty throw-upper. And I always feel sorry for myself as I am hanging over the toilet. But not party-chick Sarah. As she is throwing up, she begins to say things like, "I am an overcomer!" She throws up some more, and then says, "I will get through this!" . . . throws up more, then says, "My God loves me and is with me!" Her husband was amazed at her strength . . . here was his wife . . . in agony . . . bald . . . throwing up, and yet not whining, not giving up . . . but rather choosing to see good. She actually said later that this was a turning point for her . . . when she chose optimism over defeat.

She chose praising God over whining . . . not an easy choice! Maybe you read this and think, "Gosh, is that girl a saint or what?!?" No, she's not perfect . . . she just understands what it means to be a God chick!

Today Sarah has gotten a clean bill of health, her hair is growing back, and her physical strength is returning, but her smile, which is an incredible one, has always been there. I am thankful for all that medicine can do, but I believe it was her choice to see good, to praise God even in the hard times that truly got her through this illness.

There is power in choosing to see the good. Let's not go

through life on automatic pilot. Be aware of what is around you. My husband told this story one day in church.

> Sherlock Holmes and Dr. Watson went on a camping trip. After a good meal and a bottle of wine, they lay down for the night and went to sleep. Some hours later, Holmes awoke and nudged his faithful friend. "Watson, look up and tell me what you see." Watson replied, "I see millions and millions of stars." "What does that tell you?" Holmes asked. Watson pondered for a minute. "Astronomically, it tells me that there are millions of galaxies and potentially billions of planets. Astrologically, I observe that Saturn is in Leo. Horologically, I deduce that the time is approximately a quarter past three. Theologically, I can see that God is all-powerful and that we are small and insignificant. Meteorologically, I suspect that we will have a beautiful day tomorrow. Why, what does it tell you?" Holmes said . . . "Watson, you idiot! Someone has stolen our tent!"

Sometimes we are blind to what is going on right in our midst. Let's open our eyes! Let's look people in the eye when we are talking to them instead of looking around to see who else might be coming into the room.

The other day I was getting in my car when a homeless woman approached me. Many times, I buy the person something to eat, but this time I reached for my purse. As I was turning to hand her some money, I heard heaven whisper, *Look at her; look at her.* So I looked at her . . . I looked at her eyes and made a connection. We give people dignity when we look at them as if they are really there. Open your eyes to the people in your world.

Party chicks also open their mouths. I know you're thinking, *Whoopee!! I have this part down!* Well, there is a catch! (☺) Our mouths shouldn't be open just to be open. The writer of the book of Proverbs told us that our mouths should be open for those unable to speak for themselves; they should be open to administer justice (Proverbs 31, verses 8–9).

I love the word *justice*. It has several definitions. One is "to make right what was wrong." With our words we have the ability to instigate justice on the earth . . . or at least in our little corner of it! Martin Luther King Jr. opened his mouth, and because he did, changes were made in our country. Susan B. Anthony opened her mouth, and because she did, women now have the freedom to vote. If more people had opened their mouths back in the eighteenth century, would we even have allowed slavery in our nation? Many stood silent. If more people had had the courage to open their mouths, would Hitler have been able to carry out the destruction that he did? Too many stood silent.

At the place where you work you can actually open your mouth and administer justice. The next time you hear someone bad-mouthing someone else, why don't you open your mouth and speak out? Or how about apologizing to your children or husband when you have done something wrong? I encouraged you in Chapter 5 to open your mouth and speak to a generation of women younger than you. If we aren't willing to open our mouths and share the mistakes and the how-to's, they will be just as confused as we were! We have the ability with our mouths to make right what was wrong.

Justice also means "to render to everyone his due treatment." This can be good and bad! In the days of the Old Testament, if someone poked out your eye, you could then poke out his eye. An eye for an eye. This actually was supposed to limit retaliation. However, Jesus came and established a new kind of justice. Humanity had turned away from the love of God. They were hurting themselves and others. They were worshiping idols rather than the living God. So the planet needed to be judged. At one time in history, God judged the planet by sending a flood and basically starting over! Not my favorite method of justice! But He said He would never do that again, so there was to be a new form of rendering justice on the earth. There was sin on the earth, and it must be judged. Jesus came, and by giving up His life, He paid the price for the sins of humanity . . . whether or not humanity ever accepted His sacrifice.

Picture it like this . . . you are in a courtroom because you were caught going 150 miles per hour in a 50-mile-per-hour zone. Bad! You are in serious trouble. The judge slams down his gavel and says, "Guilty!" The fine must be paid . . . whether by monetary means or jail time. Justice demands that the fine be paid. A crime was committed; the fine must be paid. Now, let's say that after rendering the verdict of guilty, the judge steps down from his bench, walks over to the bailiff, and pays your fine for you . . . even doing the jail time if necessary.

That's what Jesus did for us . . . we were guilty, but Jesus made the choice to pay our fine for us. That's the new justice. So what does that mean for you and me today?

It means that rather than calling your friend a bad name just because she called you one, you will open your mouth with good words. It means that rather than being late to meet your friend just because she was late to meet you last time, you will do the right thing. I'm not saying this is easy . . . I'm just saying that this is the new justice we are to administer on the earth . . . and we can because we are God chicks!!!

My friend Noriko is a God chick on the journey, just as you and I are. Her husband was at work, he set down his wallet while he talked to a client, and when he reached back to get it, it was gone. Well, duh! We live in Los Angeles. What was he thinking??? And Gary did what every husband does when he can't find something . . . he called his wife!!

That was when Noriko was amazing. She and Gary had had more than a few conversations about his losing important stuff! When he called, she could have said, "I told you so." (Because she *had* told him so on a number of occasions!) But that was not what she did. She dished out the new justice . . . rather than speaking the words that perhaps he deserved, she took a deep breath and said, "I am sorry that happened, honey. Would you like me to call the credit card companies for you and cancel the cards? Is there anything else I can do?" The new justice actually involves mercy, and that was what she opened her mouth with . . . some much-needed mercy! You go, girl!

Another way we are to open our mouths, according to the last chapter of Proverbs, is with "skillful and godly Wisdom" (v. 26 AMPLIFIED). No pressure there! Most of us are great at opening our mouths with an opinion . . . and that is okay . . . when someone is actually asking for it!! However, we should be able to open them with some wisdom too!

I was on a small commuter airplane . . . you know . . . the kind where your knees are smashed against the seat in front of you and you have to keep your elbows touching your ribs if you don't want to smack the passenger seated next to you. I was one of the last to board (I was in no hurry to begin this uncomfortable flight!) and noticed as I sat down that the seat next to me was empty. I began thanking God . . . because now I had ten more inches with which to make myself very comfortable! When the flight attendant shut the plane door, I knew I was home free. Yippeeee! The seat next to me would be empty! I pulled out a book and began to read, but then I started hearing conversations from the back of the plane:

MALE VOICE: Excuse me, ma'am, but that is my seat you are sitting in.

FEMALE VOICE: Yes, I know, but I would really like to sit next to my friend. Would you be willing to take my seat? Here's my seat assignment.

SAME MALE VOICE: No problem.

After a few seconds, the talking continued . . .

Make the choice to

D
A
N
C
E

through life!

SAME MALE VOICE: Excuse me, sir, but I am supposed to be in that seat.

ANOTHER MALE VOICE: Would you mind changing with me so that I could sit next to my son?

This conversation continued through two more passengers who asked him to trade. Now I was starting to sweat because he was headed to the very coveted empty seat next to me! Within minutes, sure enough, there he was . . . about to sit next to me. He laughingly said, "Whew, I thought I was never going to get to sit down!" I gave him a stiff smile (I was still working on getting over the loss of my extra ten inches!) and proceeded to keep reading. (This is the universal sign that means, "I don't want to talk.")

The man was obviously ignorant of this universal sign because he began to talk to me. First, he asked me what kind of work I did. I always have fun with this question because I have about nine different responses. As I mentioned in an earlier chapter, I work as a teacher, pastor, author, speaker, homemaker, cheerleader, and so on. So, when asked this question, I take turns with the answer . . . just to keep life fun. Okay, so I am a little weird! (You should see the looks I get when I say that I am a cheerleader!) In fact, when flying into different countries and filling out the immigration card, I always list a different occupation. Think I can get arrested for that???! When the passenger seated next to me asked what kind of work I did, I thought for a moment about which one I was up to in my rotation of answers. I answered, "I'm a pastor." Well, his jaw dropped because honestly I don't look like a pastor. And I had to add to my answer, "Really." Then I went back to my book.

But once again he ignored the universal sign and kept talking. He said, "A pastor . . . hmm . . . I've been wanting to talk to a pastor . . . and it's funny because I had to get through four seats to get to sit next to one!" Then I got really nervous . . . not only did I have a dreaded "talker" next to me, but one who wanted to talk to a pastor. I also got nervous because I have this fear that strangers are going to want me to thoroughly explain, in Hebrew, any hidden meanings of the book of Leviticus (!) or the real difference between the Major and Minor Prophets . . . I braced myself for a difficult question. As he asked the question, I was humbled . . . I just should have known my God better than that.

He said, "My wife and I just found out that she is pregnant with triplets. Our marriage was already in a tough place, and now I'm not sure what to do. Do you have any advice on how to help my marriage?" Well, I should hope I did! Not only have I written a book of basic ways to build a marriage, but I have managed to stay married to the same man for eighteen years. I opened my mouth with wisdom and shared a few ways that he could help his marriage. Just a tip . . . with men, less is more. (And I'm not just talking about clothes!)

Most of us have paid a high price for the wisdom we have learned. We should be willing to open our mouths and share it . . . not necessarily all of our opinions, but the wisdom we have earned. Your past can help someone else on his journey . . . but only if you will open your mouth and share.

One bit of caution. When opening our mouths with wisdom . . . timing is key! A few months ago, Philip, Scott (our church administrator), and I were sitting in a courtroom waiting to sign some papers. We had a long wait in front of us while the judge was handling other cases. I was reading a book while sitting between the two men. Scott leaned over me to ask Philip a question. Philip answered, and then they began a whispered conversation. The judge heard the talking going on in his courtroom and looked at me. He said very sternly, “Lady, be quiet in my courtroom, or I will have you removed!” *I* hadn’t said a word. It had been the men talking! Scott and Philip thought it funny that I had been reprimanded for their mistake. I didn’t think it was at all funny, and I gave them *the look*. You know what look that is.

A few minutes later, a Hispanic woman walked into the courtroom. I could tell she didn’t know what to do as she headed to the court clerk. She spoke only Spanish, and the clerk couldn’t understand her. He just handed her some papers and pointed her to the seat in front of me. She sat down, looking very confused. I thought that it was perfect that she sat down in front of me because I speak Spanish fluently. I leaned over the back of her seat and started to tell her, in Spanish, how to fill out the forms. I thought I was being very helpful. Well, the judge didn’t. He looked at me and yelled, “Lady, that’s it. Leave the courtroom right now!” I couldn’t believe it! I had been trying to open my mouth with wisdom and help someone. (Philip and Scott once again got a good laugh at my expense!) So timing is key when opening your mouth!

There is a proverb that says that both life and death are in the power of the tongue. And another one says that the mouth can be a well of life and that words are as silver. I believe that the words I speak are so powerful that they can bring life or death to a situation (Proverbs 18, verse 21).

I appeared on a talk show that included a panel of women whom I had never met before. We had a great time on the show talking about different subjects and answering letters that viewers had mailed in. It was an energetic program that required quick thinking and an ability to express thoughts clearly. After the show, I complimented one of the women on her genuine style and her gentle heart. It was just a simple statement made with a smile, but I could tell she was totally taken aback as she said, "What a nice thing to say. Thank you." It wasn't hard for me to do, and my few encouraging words were a blessing to her.

Our words are powerful tools that can bring hurt or healing. Let's be determined to be the chick whose words bring life. I remember one Christmas getting a letter from a friend who lived in my city. She said that money was a little scarce for her at the moment, but she wanted to give me a present. What she gave me is just as valuable as a store-bought gift, maybe more so. She gave me the gift of words. She wrote a letter of encouragement to me, telling me which of my qualities had been a blessing to her over the years (she focused on the good ones . . . there are some!) and what she hoped for me in the future. This letter meant so much to me that I still have it! Actually I have kept quite a few of the encouraging notes I have received over the years, and on days when I am having a tough time, I pull them out and have a read!

See the good. Be the encourager. Don't be the girl who is a master at life-liposuction . . . sucking all the life out of someone. You be the one putting it in!

Watch out for being critical and impatient, expecting people to always make the right decision. We don't always get it right either, so let's dish out the encouragement we ourselves need. We are all going to fail from time to time. We are all going to make mistakes. What most of us want when we make a mistake is someone to help us up, fix what needs fixing, and encourage us on the journey once again. Those of us who find fault as if it were buried treasure need to change how we see things. It is easy to point out the mistakes someone is making. The challenge, for those of us willing to take it, is to find the good in others and give the gift of encouragement today to the people we come in contact with.

Someone asked me the question, "How can you see your spouse as God sees him when all you can see is what is not good about him?" The truth is, there are times in any marriage when the negative is the easiest to see. Perhaps after years of marriage it is easy to take each other for granted or get frustrated at the weaknesses that never change. But I would like to suggest that the good qualities that were in your spouse when you married him are still there. Maybe they are hidden, and it is your job to dig them out! The more a trait is encouraged, the more you will see it. Look for the good and you will find it.

There is such power in encouragement. People are drawn to those who encourage. Go ahead . . . be the party chick who encourages. You'd be amazed at the ripple effect that can have. It is a gift that can change lives.

Offering encouragement to someone keeps you from being self-centered . . . which all of us can be! I have come to realize that the success of my life lies in my ability to be an encouragement and a help to others. The more I encourage others, the more successful my life will be.

Most of us experience negativity from within and without each day. Some of us question whether we can do whatever it is we started out to do. If we are in a tough situation . . . a relationship, family, or job crisis . . . then an encouraging word can be the difference between giving up on the situation or hanging in there. Sometimes we are entering a new arena, facing a new, perhaps exciting challenge, and still we might wonder whether we can really do it. Encouraging words from a friend can make all the difference in the world.

A few years ago I was on a plane from Sydney to Los Angeles and found myself flying with two of my favorite girlfriends on the planet . . . lucky me!!! This trip was just after my first book, *dumb things he does/dumb things she does,* was published, and I really hadn't taken the time to celebrate. (And I do like any excuse for a celebration!) Before the plane had even taken off, we grabbed a glass and made a toast. The really great thing was that we congratulated each other on recent accomplishments. What we said wasn't shallow or flip. We took the time to say something meaningful and encouraging . . . right there in the bulkhead seat! Shanelle, an officer with the United Nations; Chris, a public speaker who has changed the lives of thousands of young people with her inspirational talks; and I are doing different things fulfilling our purposes on the earth. And we are truly excited about each other's feats. We just grabbed a few moments out of eternity to encourage each other. As I looked in their faces, I felt loved and supported in a way that motivates me to succeed. I felt as if I could conquer my part of the world. What a gift they gave me! You can do the same . . . encourage and celebrate with the people in your life. The gift you give will be priceless.

There are low spots in our lives,
but there are also high spots, and most of them have come
through encouragement from someone else.
—George M. Adams

The word *encourage* means "to put courage in," and *courage* means "facing danger in spite of fear." As we encourage people, we are saying, "Keep going! You can do it!" Recently I was embarking on a new challenge in an area I'd never done anything in before, and I was a little nervous. My friend Laura, who had just moved into a new house, has three young sons and a thousand boxes to unpack, somehow found the time to write me a note telling me that she believed in me and was confident that I would do great. And my friend LeeAnn sent me a very colorful e-mail that said, "YOU CAN DO IT!!" (She's a sanguine, and remember . . . sanguines use colors, exclamation marks, and capitals a lot!) I began my new adventure ready to succeed. How thankful I am for my encouraging friends.

Friends cherish each other's hopes.
They are kind to each other's dreams.
—Henry David Thoreau

Party chicks realize the power of their words. They open their mouths to bring justice to a situation, they open their mouths and share the wisdom they have obtained, and they open their mouths with encouragement. Encouraging words are gifts. Make it a point to be encouraging to the people in your life. If you find it hard, you are just out of practice. Why do we find it easier to point out the weaknesses we see in someone rather than finding ways we can be her cheerleader? How can we so easily point out the area someone can improve in and find it hard to tell her where she is doing a great job? Develop a reputation of being the most encouraging person on the block . . . in the office . . . in your family . . . among your friends . . . wherever!

Party chicks open their mouths with laughter. Their laughter is so real that it draws people to them. Let's be women who know how to laugh . . . at ourselves and at the funny situations we encounter. Life can be serious enough. It is crucial that we take the time to have fun . . . to laugh! Most of us do very important, rather serious things for a lot of our day . . . dealing with our jobs, our children, our husbands or boyfriends, our sick mothers-in-law, keeping the house clean, figuring out what we are going to have for dinner, cleaning up doggy poop . . . you know . . . quite a bit of serious stuff!! We need to let go every now and then.

The most wasted of all days is that during
which one has not laughed.
—NICOLAS DE CHAMFORT

I do love to laugh . . . the real laughter that makes you hold your stomach (I've heard that real laughter is as good as sit-ups . . . and much more fun, don't you think?) and makes you wipe your eyes clean of the mascara that is running down your cheeks *and* causes you to look for the nearest bathroom. (If you haven't had children, you may not understand that bathroom remark!) There have been studies done about the healing aspects of laughter. Laughter and a positive attitude bolster the immune system. Anger and stress can destroy the immune system. After he was diagnosed with a degenerative spinal disease, Norman Cousins rented comedy movies that made him laugh and then allowed him to get a couple of hours of painless sleep. Laughter is definitely healing.

A proverb declares, "A happy heart is like good medicine" (Proverbs 15:13 NCV). Laughter releases some kind of endorphin that promotes healing. So, not only does laughing feel good and create abs of steel, it also can help bring about healing!

Total absence of humor renders life impossible.

—COLETTE

C'mon, you party chick . . . love the life you have been given! Do some things with your friends that create a lightheartedness. Just do some fun things. Some people are *so* serious. It really is a drag to be around someone who takes herself too seriously. You probably have at least one quirky friend who makes you smile. Spend time with her . . . not trying to make her serious, but enjoying her ability to be carefree. Go to a silly movie together and laugh out loud. Go to a card store and read each other the funny cards. I love to do this . . . and invariably I end up passing the card to a stranger so she can enjoy the joke too!

Do some relaxing things. Get a manicure . . . or a massage . . . or a tan . . . or a coffee. Go for a run . . . or a walk. Watch the sunrise . . . or the sunset. Try a new restaurant on your girls' night out. *Have* the occasional girls' night out! Have a slumber party . . . you are never too old for slumber parties! Go shopping and try on the craziest clothes. I was in Dallas one time with my friends Kelly and Laura. We went into a store in a fairly conservative neighborhood and began putting the wildest clothes combinations on our bodies. We even photographed the fun. Days later we were still laughing at how silly we looked. And it cost nothing.

Party chicks are full of life! They live each moment as if it mattered. They celebrate the victories . . . large and small! They throw "find the joy" parties when they are feeling the pressures of life. They are determined to get out of the valley and back in the parade. They throw confetti! They open up their eyes to the world around them; they open up their mouths to bring justice and wisdom to a planet crying out for both. They laugh until they can't laugh, and then they laugh some more.

My friend Owen from New Zealand told me this story:

> An old monk had given the best part of his eighty-nine years to serving God in a monastery. His lifelong work had been to translate the original Greek/Hebrew epistles into the English language. This had been a painstaking task, making sure that every word and syllable was written with precision and great care.
>
> One day, a young novice joined the order and after several days watching the older monk and learning the skills of translating from one language to another, he asked, "Has anyone ever made a mistake in the transcripts?"
>
> The old monk looked aghast. "Oh no," he replied. "In fact, I shall go downstairs to the archives and get one of the original epistles and show you how exact our copy is."
>
> Several hours passed by and the younger monk thought, "I wonder what has become of my elder brother. Maybe he has tripped and knocked himself out, or maybe some other malady has come upon him."
>
> Passing by what seemed to be myriads of dusty old books and papers, he eventually came across the older monk, who was hunched over one of the original scrolls.

"What in heaven's name is wrong?" asked the young monk.

After what seemed like an age, the elder monk looked up and with tears rolling down his cheeks, he uttered the immortal words, "The original says celebrate!"

You and I should be celebrating life. My job on the earth is to display the nature and character of Jesus, to the best of my ability. It will definitely involve celebrating. I should live my life in such a way that people are drawn to me, not repelled. So smile, Party Chick, and live your life out loud in such a way that you lead people to their Father!

The party chick is within you . . . let her out!!!

To know the true
value of time,
we must seize and enjoy
every moment of it.

—Chesterfield

Love never fails

—New Testament, 1 Corinthians 13, verse 8

CHAPTER SEVEN

the lover chick . . .

As I spread my loving arms across the land.

—Helen Reddy

Perhaps the title of this chapter sounds a little risqué! (Well, that's just the kind of girl I am!) We are to be the lovers on the earth! We truly have the God-given capacity for it. I believe that we are to be so great at loving that our planet is the better for it. Although this might sound a bit lofty, we actually practice this loving in our own backyards. It is easy to say, "I love people," but we live that out by loving the people who come across our path every day.

I am here to serve my generation. Jesus served His and, in turn, affected every generation afterward. He turned the world upside down through love. In spite of the suffering and the rejection He endured, He continued to love. I'm not sure I am to do any less. I am to serve my generation by loving it. I am to be the lover chick with my heart open to love.

We should become great at loving . . . loving humanity . . . our husbands . . . our children . . . our friends . . . our God. We are the lover chicks! Pure love is based not on what my husband, friends, or even God can do for me, but on what I can do for them. Loving humanity involves seeing humanity, which I talked about in the last chapter. We can't turn a blind eye to the pain and suffering going on around us. And yet we might watch a TV show that documents some group of hurting people on the other side of the earth and feel powerless to bring change. Rather than feeling this sense of powerlessness, how about demonstrating our love for hurting humanity by loving the hurting ones in our own neighborhoods? And I would wager that most of us won't have to look very far to find hurting people.

I am to be the lover chick with my heart open to love.

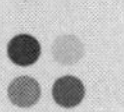

My friend Shanelle says it like this: "Jesus' message of love and hope was a global one, but He lived it out locally." If each of us takes care of loving her own corner of the world, the world ought to be a terrific place! You can certainly travel to far-off lands and help where needed, but I also hope to encourage you to help that single mom with HIV who lives in your community or give groceries to that family whose dad lost his job and the mom is sick. We have something we can give . . . some way in which we can touch someone who is hurting . . . and we probably won't have to get on a plane to do it! (Although I have found that if you are faithful to love the neighborhood you are in, then God often opens up other neighborhoods.)

> *You will find as you look back upon your life that the moments that you have really lived, are the moments when you have done things in the spirit of love.*
>
> —Henry Drummond

If we are going to love people, we have to keep our hearts open. Most of us, at one time or another, have experienced betrayal. We have been let down by people, and we have probably been hurt. If we are not careful, we will let bitterness settle in our hearts and shut them down. We could grow into angry, twisted, sad, old women if we let bitterness live in our hearts. That is not the picture I want of myself!

My friend Lisa Peacock had a father who died in a plane crash when she was nine. Her mom died in a car accident when Lisa was nineteen. She was angry and bitter for a few years. And that's understandable. Then she did what others have a hard time doing. She made the decision to let go of the bitterness. Yes, there was still pain, but she made the choice to keep her heart open. As a young person, she found that she had gotten very little help in dealing with the pain of losing her father and then her mother. She recognized that there was a need to help children deal with bereavement, and so now, at twenty-three, she has started a nonprofit organization that helps children deal with loss. She has taken counseling classes . . . bereavement classes . . . and is getting the training necessary to be successful at what she wants to do, which is to help hurting children. (Check out her Web site www.peacockfoundation.org.) She is loving humanity by loving the children in her corner of the earth. She is being a lover chick!! You go, girl!

My mother is a real lover chick. (How do you like that title, Mom?) She lives in Texas and recently met a twenty-year-old single mom. This young woman got pregnant while in high school and lost a sports scholarship to go to college. Her family basically disowned her, and now she is working multiple jobs to support herself and her child. She managed to get her GED, but would really like to go to college. She doesn't see that she will be able to. She's barely making ends meet with the jobs she has now. And she probably *wouldn't* get the chance to go except that *now* she has met my mother . . . who is a real mother. My mother has decided to open her heart and extend herself on behalf of this young woman. With my mother's help the young woman could be going to junior college and getting the degree she wants. My mom is simply loving humanity by loving a young woman in her community.

My friend Nancy Alcorn is the founder and president of

Mercy Ministries. After working with troubled youths since 1973, she was determined to establish a program in which lives would truly be transformed, and so in 1983, she founded Mercy Ministries of America. Mercy is truly a remarkable place. Presently there are three residential facilities in the U.S. and one in Australia, and plans are under way to open additional homes in the U.S. and abroad. She continues to run the organization without government funding because she wants to be able to teach the girls about their loving Creator and the Savior who died for them. In these homes, girls come, completely free of charge, to a place so filled with love that change is inevitable. Young women who are battling eating disorders or dealing with teenage pregnancies, depression, or sexual dysfunction are welcomed into a loving environment where they are taught about the God who loves them. Women, whom the world had given up on, begin the life they were destined to live. The success stories that come out of these homes are remarkable. Nancy Alcorn is truly a lover chick, and it all began because she loved the girls in her neighborhood and saw a way she could help. Now her neighborhood has expanded to include more of the world. Recently Nancy met with President Bush, and he called her a "soldier in the army of compassion." I love that! (Check out what's going on with Nancy at www.mercyministries.org.)

I also want to make one other point to all of you over forty-year-olds who are reading this book. (Thanks, by the way!) Millions of young girls around the world have no idea what it means to have a mother's love and support. Regardless of your own past, which in itself might have been painful . . . and I am sorry for that . . . I am asking you to please extend yourself to a generation that so desperately needs you. Find a young woman in your community who might be struggling, and offer to help. Sometimes just a shoulder to cry on and an ear that listens are enough.

And for you young women . . . I'm sorry if you have been let down by a woman who should have loved and cared for you. I'm sorry if you didn't have a mother who openly talked with you about life . . . its ups and downs. Please don't let yourself become bitter. I believe that there will be an older woman who will extend herself to you. And also keep in mind that you have a job! There are younger girls . . . those who are now in elementary school . . . who will one day be looking to you to help them. So keep your heart open . . . because there are girls who need you to.

Find a young woman in your community who might be struggling, and offer to help.

If every generation of women would look out for the one younger, offering help and imparting wisdom, we would truly have a healthy population of women!

How about you? Is there someone in your neighborhood who could use a friend . . . who could use a helping hand? You probably won't have to look very far. We have set up a tutoring program at our church that allows us to love our corner of Los Angeles by helping kids with their homework. Maybe you could drive an older person to the grocery store; maybe you could baby-sit for a single mom; maybe you could become a foster parent; maybe you could make dinner for a new mom . . . there are lots of simple ideas of how to love humanity. I am sure you could think of plenty more.

As lover chicks, we are also to be great at loving our families . . . loving our husbands, children, and parents. Most of us begin a marriage still riding high on that euphoric, dreamlike, in-love feeling. This kind of love is the cloudy, floaty feeling that has no basis in reality! While you are in this state, you are incredibly altruistic. You will do whatever your boyfriend/spouse wants to do. You go to *every* sporting event he wants. You watch the games on TV with him. You see movies where a lot of people are blown up and there are long car chases. And he is fairly altruistic during this phase as well. He takes long walks on the beach or in the park. He goes to movies where there is a lot of crying. He meets all three hundred members of the family. He is happy just to hold you. Remember those days! (☺)

During this phase of love, you can't think of one thing wrong with your boyfriend/spouse. You see only the good, and you ignore any warning that friends or family might bring up. The problem with this kind of love is that it is not the everlasting kind . . . it generally lasts two years or so, and by this time, you are probably well and truly married. It is at this time as the

We can do something extraordinary, by doing something ordinary with love—"just one day at a time."

—Lucinda Vardey

euphoric "in-love" feeling dissipates that many couples will say, "I married the wrong person," or "I'm just not in love anymore, and I want out."

We have all had those feelings at some point in a marriage. Don't get discouraged about your marriage if you have—or have had—those feelings. You just now have the opportunity to build the love that will last a lifetime, and it is not determined by what you feel as much as by what you do. Real love is not a place you fall into; it is not a feeling; it is what you *do* . . . sometimes in spite of what you are feeling.

I love my husband more now, after eighteen years of marriage, than I ever did. And there was a time in the beginning of our marriage when that euphoric, fluffy, in-love phase left, and I just didn't feel any love toward him. (I'm sure he was questioning his feelings too!) There was a time when I wanted *out* of this marriage . . . because he just wasn't making me happy (as if that is anyone else's job but mine!). He was no longer a prince or charming, and I was ready to throw the shoe at him! (Anybody ever been there?) But instead of leaving, I made the decision to work on our marriage . . . I got some help. Together, Philip and I learned to build the love that we know will see us through to the end of our lives . . . actually we work on it all the time. Sometimes I look back at what I almost gave up and shudder to think of the love I almost threw away . . . the real kind of love.

As a lover chick, love your husband. If the feelings aren't there right now, then *do* loving things. Feelings will follow. Forgive, touch, make a meal, watch TV with him, say nice things . . . ask him what makes him feel loved, then do those things. (Believe it or not, it probably is more than sex!) Love is all about communicating . . . verbal as well as physical.

Learn how to be great at communicating to your man. It is definitely different from talking to your girlfriend . . . only most of us talk to our husbands as if they were girlfriends! We have to stop that! Your husband probably doesn't want to hear about your whole journey through the mall . . . just how much it cost him! Give him the headlines . . . if he wants to know more, he'll ask for it. I have heard some women talk to their husbands as if they were their mothers. Not good! If you start to talk to him as if he is a boy . . . he will act like one, and that is probably not what you want!

Your husband's number-one need is to feel respected . . . he equates love with respect, so your job in communicating to him is to make sure you are communicating respect. Sometimes you may communicate by demanding or by blasting forth with unasked-for opinions. Not very respectful. Proverbs 31:26 declares, "She opens her mouth with wisdom, and on her tongue is the law of kindness." *Kindness* literally means "loyalty." The words you use should show loyalty to your husband. When you're loyal to someone, you demonstrate that you're on the same team. A surefire way for me to start a fight with Philip is to come into a conversation, attacking with both guns blazing! (I always carry at least one!) What this proverb is asking me to do is to approach my husband as if we are on the same team. Philip is not my enemy (no matter how many times it has felt that way). He and I should be on the same team, fighting a common enemy—not each other.

Listening is probably the most important aspect of loving communication.

Look at your heart: Do you secretly feel that you are on the opposite team from your husband? Begin to change that. Do you secretly (or perhaps not so secretly!) roll your eyes at some of the decisions he makes? That is a pretty demeaning method of communicating. Demonstrate respect by working together to overcome a problem. Demonstrate respect by being loyal.

Listening is probably the most important aspect of loving communication. Women are amazing! Because of the way our brains are formed, we can quickly go from left-brain functions to right-brain functions . . . no problem. Men, on the other hand, are not quite so adept at this. We are much better at multitasking. For example, we can have a conversation on the phone, work at the computer, and braid our daughter's hair—all at the same time. Easy. Not so for our husbands. If Philip is having a conversation with me, the truth is, I can do something else at the same time . . . such as cooking or playing a game with my daughter or doing my nails. However, because he is not a great multitasker, he thinks I am not listening to him. So, because I want to communicate respect to him, and because I want him to know I am really listening, I stop what I am doing and give him my undivided attention. He feels loved and listened to, and after all, isn't that the goal of communicating?

Great marriages are built over a lifetime, so don't give up. Maybe you are on marriage number two or three . . . well, make this the one with which you finish out life. Do different things in this one. Read books about relationships, spend time with couples committed to their relationship, and commit to making the *we* more important than the *me*.

In the book of Proverbs, we learn that the woman of valor, the God chick, does her husband good and not evil all the days of her life. Interestingly enough, in chapter 31, the husband is described as sitting in the gates of the city. That was a position of influence. Most of the chapter discusses the awesome woman, but there is this one sentence noting the husband's position of influence in the city. Even though it seems out of place, I don't think it is. I think that the wife had a lot to do with the position of authority the husband had. I think he got that position because of the way his wife talked about him . . . the way she demonstrated respect to him. I think it is possible that he achieved his position because of how she loved him.

Most of us want our husbands to be successful in their chosen careers . . . and I think it is possible to love them to success. I have certainly heard some women complain and be so critical of their husbands that it seems to strip the men of any authority and power whatsoever. Their husbands are probably not sitting in the gates of the city. What do you think?

I want my husband to feel safe with me. I want to be a safe

place for him to unwind . . . for him to share dreams and fears. I want him to feel safe in sharing feelings, knowing that I won't be offended. I truly want to be an uncomplicated person in his life. I want him to breathe a sigh of relief when I walk into the room, knowing that his friend, his partner, his cheerleader, his lover is here.

Lover chicks love their children. I used to think that this kind of love was natural, and of course, every woman loved her children! But increasingly I meet young women whose mothers abandoned them after they met a new man who didn't want life "cluttered" by children. That is why we have to be prepared to mother a young woman who might not be ours by blood. In your community, I promise you, there is a young woman who needs a little mothering.

Lover chicks communicate that love freely and regularly to their children. Tell your children (no matter their age) that you love them. Hug them. Spend time with them. Give them direction, and at the same time give them room to grow. Don't try to make them into your image. Tell them the truth about life with its rewards and challenges. Talk about sex. Talk about drugs. Listen to their music with them. Realize they will be affecting a generation different from your own, and empower them to do that. (Don't try to make them dress as if they are living in the fifties . . . unless, of course, that is the new trend! ☺) When they drive you nuts, try really hard to focus on the good things you see in them! Even when it's hard . . . don't abandon them . . . either physically or emotionally.

In loving my children, I had to realize that my son, Jordan (age sixteen), and my daughter, Paris (age eleven), were quite different from each other. As Gary Chapman has said in his many books, people have different love languages. My daughter feels loved when I spend time with her. She loves nothing more than to cuddle on the bed and watch a video, or to be in the swimming pool with me and play games. One weekend Philip and Jordan were out of town, and she and I had the house to ourselves. We went to the movies, then we came home and got in the Jacuzzi, where we had the most interesting discussion about male and female body parts! (I just wished I could have recorded the conversation to play when she is all grown up!) Then we got in my bed and watched yet another movie before I read her a book. So, all in all, we spent forty-eight straight hours together. Her love tank was full!

My son, however, is a bit different. While most of the time he enjoys my company, he actually feels loved by physical affection. It is a little trickier now to express it than when he was younger, but I still squeeze him whenever I can. I'll pat him on the shoulder or grab his arm as he dashes past. Sometimes at night, I will sit next to him and rub his back. I have had to get more creative as he has gotten older and doesn't really want to be seen hugging his mom! Oh, well, c'est la vie! And as a teenager, he is just different . . . is that putting it mildly!?! Sometimes I feel as if I am on an emotional roller coaster, which is not a lot of fun. And there have been times when I have wanted to throw my hands up in frustration, but because

I love him, I stay committed to the journey of being his mother. I'm sure one day he will be thrilled!

Lover chicks love their friends. I spent a whole chapter on how to be a good friend chick . . . and it is such a passion of mine . . . to see us get good at the girlfriend thing. Take a moment right now and write a short note to a friend . . . even if you saw her today . . . tell her how important she is to you. You could very well make her day!

Lover chicks love their God! So how do we let the Creator of the universe know that we love Him? Well, we can tell Him! That's one way we let others know we love them—by opening our mouths and telling them . . . so I'm pretty sure it would work for God too! And then we demonstrate our love for Him by what we do. How do we do that? By loving each other! The apostle John said it like this: "If someone says, 'I love God,' and hates his brother, he is a liar; for he who does not love his brother whom he has seen, how can he love God whom he has not seen?" (1 John 4:20). So once again, it all comes down to loving people! We demonstrate our love for God by loving the people He puts in our lives. Eugene Peterson put it like this:

> My beloved friends, let us continue to love each other since love comes from God. Everyone who loves is born of God and experiences a relationship with God. The person who refuses to love doesn't know the first thing about God, because God is love—so you can't know him if you don't love. This is how God showed his love for us: God sent his

> only Son into the world so we might live through him. This is the kind of love we are talking about—not that we once upon a time loved God, but that he loved us and sent his Son as a sacrifice to clear away our sins and the damage they've done to our relationship with God. My dear, dear friends, if God loved us like this, we certainly ought to love each other. No one has seen God, ever. But if we love one another, God dwells deeply within us, and his love becomes complete in us—perfect love! (1 John 4:7–12 *THE MESSAGE*)

Jesus came for two reasons . . . to reconcile us back to our Creator and to reconcile us to each other. Because of what Jesus did, we have the ability to love, and by loving each other, we love God. How cool is that?!!

So . . . lover chicks love humanity by loving their corner of it . . . they love their husbands . . . their children . . . their friends . . . and by doing all of that loving, they are actually loving God. Let's be the lovers on the earth! (Maybe we should get T-shirts made!?)

Love sought is good,
but given unsought is better.
—William Shakespeare

You will find as you look back upon your life that the moments that you have really lived are the moments when you have done things in the spirit of love.

—Henry Drummond

CHAPTER EIGHT

the whatever-it-takes chick . . .

If a man is called to be a street sweeper, he should sweep streets even as Michelangelo painted or Beethoven composed music or Shakespeare wrote poetry. He should sweep streets so well that all the hosts of heaven and earth will pause to say, "Here lived a street sweeper who did his job well."

—MARTIN LUTHER KING JR.

Sometimes I feel as if I should join the circus. No, I can't tame elephants (although I can have a conversation with a teenage boy, so that's pretty close!). No, I can't ride horses while standing in a feathered tutu (although I can navigate the traffic of Los Angeles!). No, I can't contort my body to fit in a shoe box . . . but

I *am* a champion plate spinner! I have so many plates spinning that I amaze myself. Can you relate? Most of you probably can. I have the woman plate going, the wife plate going, the mom plate going, the pastor plate going, the author plate going, the speaker plate going, and the friend plate going. And each plate has a few smaller plates orbiting it.

One Thursday I was taking a shower and feeling just a bit overwhelmed with life. I was scheduled to teach our weekend services (there are four of them) and had to prepare a message in the next day or so. Both Jordan and Paris had basketball games, and of course, I was the snack mom. Paris had a test in science the next day and needed help studying. I was going out of the country the following Tuesday to speak at a conference; my friend was going through a rough patch and needed some coffee time with me; my publisher wanted another chapter of a book by Friday . . . and . . . I'm sure my husband wanted sex and a hot meal somewhere in this picture!!

So I started moaning and crying to God about all the plates I was spinning. I was trying to get God to feel sorry for me too. But it didn't work. I heard heaven say, *Which of those plates do you want to drop?* I thought for a minute and realized that I didn't want to drop any of them. I love all the aspects of my life. Then I heard, *Well, you better get great at spinning them because there are even more coming your way!*

There is much I want to do on the earth, much I want to accomplish. Often I will find myself asking God for more . . . more increase . . . more provision . . . more blessing. Although that is not necessarily wrong, I think the better prayer is, "God, make *me* bigger . . . increase *me*" (and I am not talking about the size of my hips!). By now, most of us have probably heard of the prayer of Jabez. In this prayer, Jabez asked God to bless him and enlarge his territory. Enlarging your territory means enlarging your area of responsibility, so be careful when you pray that! You are asking for another plate to spin! Yikes!

But the truth is, God needs us to be great at handling more and more. He needs each of us to be the whatever-it-takes chick. We can't be the ones wilting under pressure. We can't be the ones decreasing in passion or ability. The King of heaven is counting on us to do our part, and it definitely involves growing and stretching. We have to be the ones who will do whatever it takes to get the job done.

Jesus told a parable about a man who went on a trip. Before he left, he got his three servants together and gave five thousand dollars to one, two thousand dollars to another one, and one thousand dollars to the last one. He gave each a different amount according to his ability to handle it. He wasn't playing favorites. The one who had been given the five thousand dollars wisely invested it, and it doubled. The one who had been given two thousand also doubled his money. However, the man with one thousand dollars buried his money in the ground and did nothing with it. The employer came back and rewarded the two who doubled what they had been given. He then became angry with the one who had not tried to grow or increase what had been given to him. So the employer took the one thousand away from him and gave it to the one who had proved he knew how to increase.

There are a few lessons I have learned from this parable. The first is that we are given resources, either gifts or money, based on our ability to handle them. In the parable, the five-thousand-dollar guy had a five-thousand-dollar ability or capacity. The one-thousand- dollar guy had a one-thousand-dollar ability or capacity. Sometimes we are asking God for more, and if He did give us more, we wouldn't be able to contain it because we don't have the capacity. I have read stories of people who have won millions of dollars in the lottery, and yet in a few years they have lost most of it because they didn't have the capacity to handle millions. Maybe they had the capacity to handle thousands but not millions.

We are given resources, either gifts or money, based on our abilities to handle them.

As a parent, I don't give my kids more than they can handle. They always *want* more than they can handle (kind of like us!). But I will not give the car keys to my eleven-year-old daughter, no matter what, no matter how many times she asks. Why? Is it because I am a mean mother? No. I know she would hurt herself and others if she got behind a wheel now. She doesn't have the ability to drive a car yet. Eventually, however, after she has taken driver's education and turned sixteen and I have purchased lots of insurance (!), I will give them to her. Her capacity will have increased.

The whatever-it-takes chick knows that God wants to bless her and give her all that she needs to fulfill her purpose on the earth. He is not withholding anything. The only one stopping her from having what she needs is her. If she is going to be able to contain what heaven wants to give her, then she must increase her ability to contain it. The five-thousand-dollar guy increased his capacity from five to ten. He is now a ten-thousand-dollar guy. The two-thousand-dollar guy also increased his capacity. He is now a four-thousand-dollar guy. God will now give each of them resources based on their new capacities. The one-thousand-dollar guy didn't increase his capacity, and so his resource was taken away . . . not his capacity . . . just his resource, so he will get another chance as a one-thousand-dollar guy.

The whatever-it-takes chick takes care of what she has been given, stewarding it well so that her capacity will be increased. If you and I want abundance in anything . . . marriage, finances, talent, friendships, career . . . it starts with taking care of what we now have. If I use what is given to me, I will be given more. If I fail to use what has been given to me, even what I have will be taken away.

We have to be great at developing what has been given to us. We are not to feel frustrated by what we have today, but manage it!

One of Ripley's "Believe It or Not" items pictured a plain

bar of iron worth $5. The same bar of iron made into horseshoes would be worth $50. If it were made into needles, it would be worth $5,000. If it were made into balance springs for fine Swiss watches, it would be worth $500,000. The raw material is not as important as how it's developed.

Don't get frustrated at your minimum-wage job, but be the best employee. Whether in physical, intellectual, financial, or relational dealings, whatever is given to you, however small it is, use it—and use it diligently. This diligence will increase your capacity to handle an even better job. Don't ask for a bigger, better job until you are great at the one you have.

Don't ask for a bigger, better job until you are great at the one you have.

Sometimes girls will look at me and say, "I want what you have." And I know they are talking about the lifestyle . . . which involves a healthy marriage and family, a calling on the earth that is rewarding, and friends around the planet. I know they are looking at a twenty-year result and wanting it instantly. So I say, "Well, study hard . . . read a book a week . . . stay married when you feel like leaving . . . write a letter to a friend when you'd rather shop . . . play with your children when you want some time alone . . . write when you feel like sleeping . . . work out when you feel like playing . . . control emotions when you feel like screaming . . . forgive when you feel like hating . . . overcome limitations when you want to quit. Do those things and you will have what I have. There is no magic to it. I have just been a good steward over what has been given to me, and so my capacity has increased. Yours will too."

If we are committed to being whatever-it-takes chicks . . . increasing our capacity and our ability to handle more . . . then we must spend time with people who help enlarge us. Whom are you spending time with? Whom are you having coffee with? Spend time with people who are also committed to being enlarged . . . those who will learn from you or those you will learn from.

Be careful how much time you spend with bitter, negative, critical people. Their world is very small. Their capacity is tiny, and it will not help you enlarge yours.

If I am going to increase my capacity to love (and I better do that), if I am going to increase my capacity to forgive (and I better do that), if I am going to increase my capacity to give (and I better do that), I need to spend time with people who are loving more, forgiving more, and giving more.

The whatever-it-takes chick is also increasing her ability to do more, so I need to spend time with people who are committed to doing. It doesn't help me to hear people say, "Poor you! How do you handle all those plates you are spinning? You should set some down." I need to spend time with people who say, "Good for you . . . keep on going! Need some help?"

God isn't looking down from heaven and feeling sorry for me

spinning all my plates. He is looking way down the road and sees the place where I am headed and knows that I need to be enlarging, so He is saying, "Come on, Holly, get good at what is in your life now because I have so much more for you. I have people farther down the road that I need you to touch . . . so keep growing!"

No one wants me to live in abundance more than God does. He wants me to continually increase my capacity . . . to grow so that He can give me more . . . so that I can do more. Just a word of caution to all of us plate spinners out there: I am assuming that the plates you are spinning are the ones that are on your path of purpose . . . the ones in the lane you are running. If you are spinning a plate you are not supposed to, well, you definitely better put that one down because you will be fulfilled enough with all the plates you are supposed to be spinning!

No one wants me to live in abundance more than God does.

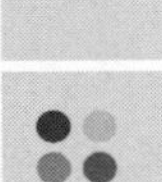

The God chick of Proverbs 31 bought and sold businesses without neglecting her present duties. Basically she was given more plates to spin, and she managed to spin them without dropping the ones she had. She picked up the new plates because as a whatever-it-takes chick, she would do whatever was needed to see that the purpose she had been given was fulfilled. She managed to see to her household with all that required without whining or feeling self-pity. She probably never had a complaining-to-God shower experience! Oh, well, I haven't had that many!

At this time in history, Laura Bush has significant influence. But it didn't start here. She went to a university and got a degree in education. Then she began teaching. Next, she got a master's degree in library science and continued teaching. It is evident by what she chose to spend her time doing that she loves children, learning, and books. She married George W. Bush, who became governor of Texas. She served on advisory boards that had to do with education and reading. Her influence continued to increase. After her husband was elected president of the United States, her capacity was increased. She started a national initiative called Ready to Read, Ready to Learn. She urged more Americans to become teachers and discussed, on a national level, how we can better prepare young children for learning and school. In 2001, she launched the first National Book Festival, which showcased authors from across the nation and was attended by thousands of people. Since the attacks of September 11, she has focused her energy on helping our nation, especially the children, through the healing process. In May of 2002, she addressed the plight of the children and women of Afghanistan by speaking to them from Prague in a radio address that reached Afghanistan. She let them know that we were with them and would do what we could to help.

There is a purpose behind this little biography lesson! Right now Laura Bush has the platform to speak to millions of women around the world. She has the ability to launch programs that will help millions of children with basic needs as well as education. She started her journey, not with the capacity she has now, but with a much smaller one. She was just a girl growing up in Texas, who was faithful to take care of what she had been given. She had the opportunity to go to a university and graduate school, so rather than goofing off, she did the best she could. She accomplished her educational goals. Then she began to work and influence the children in her community. Not the world yet, just her community. When she was the governor's wife, she worked on educational issues and promoted women's health issues. Now, as the president's wife, she has a global platform to bring help to women and children around the earth. Because she had been faithful to grow what was given to her, her capacity increased, and she is able to do what God would have her do at this time in history.

The world of the generous gets larger and larger.

—PROVERBS 11:24 (THE MESSAGE)

Whatever-it-takes chicks must be great at handling pressure. The truth is, in life, there will always be varying degrees of pressure that we may feel. I would like to suggest that pressure itself isn't bad . . . in fact, there is power under pressure. I'm sure many of you have played with a windup toy. You probably have one from McDonald's under your car seat right now! The goal of a windup toy is for the toy to move. The toy moves only when you wind it. (This is deep, I know!) The winding causes pressure, or tension, that when released moves the toy. So the pressure did a good thing! A steam engine was designed to work by letting off steam, which was produced by a buildup of pressure caused by heat. Again, the pressure did a good thing. Diamonds are formed by time and lots of pressure being put on carbon. We all want the sparkly diamond . . . and it became the diamond by enduring lots of pressure. So pressure itself isn't bad. The key is what we do when we are under pressure.

Pressure can make us do stupid things. Samson, the memorable muscle man of the Old Testament, felt lots of pressure. Delilah pressured him to reveal what he wasn't supposed to. Under the pressure, he caved in, and it cost him dearly.

After high school, I went to Duke University and had a tremendous first semester as a freshman. I made the dean's list and had a very high GPA. At that point in my life, I had plans to go to medical school, and so I was putting a lot of pressure on myself to get straight A's, or at least pretty close. The second semester was a bit tougher academically. I got back a test one day in biology, and rather than the A I was hoping for, I got a C. Not good. I looked at the test and realized that I had made a stupid mistake in a diagram. I was so frustrated at myself that I took my eraser and changed the answer I put on the test to be the right answer. What do you call that? I'm pretty sure it is called cheating! This class had a policy that you could submit your test for a regrade if you thought it had been graded incorrectly. I submitted the paper to be regraded after I changed the answer.

Well, this class also had a policy of making random copies of some of the students' original tests, just to make sure that no one was taking unfair advantage of the regrade policy. Guess whose paper just "happened" to be one of the ones that had been copied? You guessed it . . . mine. So my professor had proof that I had cheated, and he called me into his office. Duke doesn't take cheating very lightly, and it was only because the dean of students said to give me another chance that I was allowed to stay in school.

I didn't handle the pressure very well. Like Samson, I was under pressure that caused me to make a very poor decision. Because we are alive at this time on the planet, and because the job that heaven has given us to do is an awesome one, we will experience pressure. I suggest that you not buckle under pressure; rather, let it take you to the next level. Let it wind you up to move on, or let it cause you to proceed full steam ahead!

I suggest that you not buckle under pressure; rather, let it take you to the next level.

What do you do when you are under pressure in your marriage? Do you take it out on your spouse . . . blaming him? Do you just want to quit, saying, "This is too hard"? Or do you let the pressure drive you to your knees in prayer? Do you read a book about marriage . . . hang out with a happily married couple? Are you willing to make needed changes?

What do you do when you are under pressure in your health? Are you willing to change how you eat or exercise? Are you going to whine about how unfair it is . . . or are you, like the woman who had been bleeding for twelve years, going to press in until you touch the Healer?

What do you do when you are under pressure in your finances? Do you panic? Do you quit being generous? Do you keep your faith in God, or do you shake your fist at Him? Or do you let the pressure drive you to learn some things about budgeting and money management?

When you are under pressure, do you hold back, cry, get sick, yell at people, freak out, panic? Well, you can do all those things at first, but then you must make a different decision. Sometimes under pressure we say things that are very damaging, so be careful about what you are letting out of your mouth.

Whatever-it-takes chicks do whatever is needful at the time. I have the privilege of working with some pretty incredible God chicks. At our regular God chick meetings, we are all committed to seeing God's purpose done . . . with seeing girls have a life-changing experience. This kind of meeting doesn't come off just because we want it to. No, a lot of work is involved. These girls give up hours and hours of their free time to help set up, clean up, and prepare. They are there early to greet our guests and just to offer a friendly smile! They stay late to make sure the building is clean.

They empty trash bags and clean candle wax off the carpet. (Having very large candelabras over our new carpet was not one of my better ideas . . . but my whatever-it-takes chick friends cleaned up the mess my idea caused . . . thank you . . . thank you . . . thank you!) Some of them are very comfortable on the stage singing, acting, dancing, or being the emcee. (A lot of them do it for a living.) But I know that if I handed them the toilet brush instead of the microphone, they would gladly clean the toilet because they are whatever-it-takes chicks. And these chicks have no ego. They know it is not about them; rather, it is about the purpose of heaven. So whether you are given a broom, dish towel, or microphone . . . do your part and do it with all your heart.

Whatever-it-takes chicks don't look for what is the least they can do. No, they go the extra mile. Whatever-it-takes chicks are not stingy. No, they are the generous ones on the planet. Their hands are filled and open so that they can give of what they have. The fully awesome God chick of Proverbs 31 is likened to a merchant ship. That is not talking about her shape . . . aren't you glad?? It is talking about her function. Merchant ships brought goods from around the world. You and I are to be vessels filled with good things so that we can give them away.

If we want to continually be filled, then we must understand about giving. When we give of what is in our hands to give, then our hands are filled up again. Paul wrote it like this:

> Remember this: [she] who sows sparingly and grudgingly will also reap sparingly and grudgingly, and [she] who sows

> generously that blessings may come to someone will also reap generously and with blessings. Let each one give as [she] has made up [her] own mind and purposed in [her] heart, not reluctantly or sorrowfully or under compulsion, for God loves (He takes pleasure in, prizes above other things, and is unwilling to abandon or to do without) a cheerful (joyous, "prompt to do it") giver whose heart is in [her] giving. And God is able to make all grace (every favor and earthly blessing) come to you in abundance, so that you may always and under all circumstances and whatever the need be self-sufficient possessing enough to require no aid or support and furnished in abundance for every good work and charitable donation . . . Thus you will be enriched in all things and in every way, so that you can be generous, and your generosity as it is administered by us will bring forth thanksgiving to God. (2 Cor. 9:6–8, 11 AMPLIFIED)

Being generous is my decision. I refuse to let someone else decide my generosity. So let's be givers of what has been given to us!! You and I as God chicks on the planet should be the best givers of what we have to give . . . be it money or time or friendship or encouragement or love or patience or . . . the list goes on and on!

Think about it. If you are having friends over for dinner, and unexpectedly they bring an out-of-town visitor . . . and you had only enough steaks for the guests you had planned on . . . who will do without? You will . . . I would. And we would do our best

> *You and I as God chicks on the planet should be the best givers of what we have to give.*

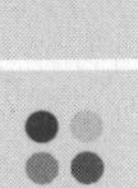

not to frown about it! We are naturally givers. If our kids need something, we do whatever we can to see that they get it . . . we might even go without so that they could have what they need. Why? Because we are givers. I'm trying to help you see that it is a God-given quality . . . He created us to be the givers on the planet. He trusts us to be His funnels. He trusts us to give of what we have been given and not to be hoarders.

Our posture to the world should be with our hands filled, open, and extended to those who need what we have. You and I are created to be givers! We have been given an amazing Savior . . . we are supposed to be introducing Him to others . . . we have been given a future and a hope . . . we are supposed to be giving hope to others . . . we have been entrusted with a destiny . . . we are supposed to be living it out in such a way that lives are touched.

The whatever-it-takes chick opens her hands and uses them to do good on the planet. There are actually two terms that are used when translating the word *hand*. One of them is used to describe the hand that gives and is extended to pray for others. I've talked about that hand. The other term refers to the hand that wars. Now, before you pick up a machine gun, let me give you a picture of warring hands because we have to be careful how we interpret this. Yes, we have an enemy . . . the devil . . . and he would love to keep the woman down. So my hands must be extended and ready to do spiritual battle . . . ready to defeat fear, discouragement, or strife. We absolutely need to be able and ready to wield our spiritual swords and bravely subdue the plans of the enemy.

However, I have to say that sometimes it would be easier to wave my fists and yell at the devil than it would be to use my hands and make dinner for my husband, especially if he has made me mad, and yet that is warfare. Sometimes it might be easier to yell and wave my fists in anger at the poverty in our city than it would be to use my hands to make a sandwich to give to a hungry person. Sometimes warfare is extending my hands with love when what I want to do is to extend them with something to throw in them!

Recently Philip and I had a disagreement. (Okay, we had a fight.) My feelings were hurt, and I wanted to walk out of the room being the martyr. (I can really play that part.) And I am great at dramatic exits. He had said some things he shouldn't have, and I got defensive rather than try to listen. Basically what we had was a mess. Anybody ever been there?? But since I was working out this open-hand thing, I figured I had better practice what I preach. Sometimes that is *so* hard!! So, rather than storming out of the room or throwing something at him, I opened my hand (it had been clenched into a fist!) and reached for his. He held my hand,

and the fight pretty much ended. That was warfare—extending my hand in love and forgiveness when I wanted to do something else with it.

The whatever-it-takes chick is pretty amazing. She is great at spinning the plates she is supposed to be spinning. She continues to increase her capacity, thus expanding her sphere of influence. She doesn't buckle under pressure. She lets the pressure propel her to the next level. She does whatever is needed, without ego involved, to accomplish the task in front of her. She generously opens her filled hands and gives of what she has . . . be it love, time, kindness, or a financial resource. The world needs you to release the whatever-it-takes chick residing inside you!

Now join your hands,
and with your hands your
hearts.

—William Shakespeare

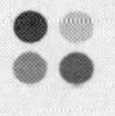

a final challenge for the God chicks out there . . .

You really can change the world if you care enough.

—MARIAN WRIGHT EDELMAN

Each of the chapters, I hope, has brought a colorful description of the awesome and amazing women we are. Once we truly understand just who we are, our job is to influence our world with it. Although women in Afghanistan are shedding their burkas, millions of women around the world have not been blessed with the liberation that most of us take for granted. Some young girls in India and Southeast Asia are still sold into brothels so that their families can avoid having to feed one more mouth. Millions of baby girls in China were aborted or murdered simply because they were female. Some cultures still don't educate girls, feeling that they are inferior to boys. So you and I have a job to do. Interestingly enough, if you look at a map of the world's most poverty- and disease-stricken spots, and you overlay it with a map of the parts of the world where women are the most oppressed, you will find them to be identical. A nation can't oppress half of God's children and expect to be blessed.

On behalf of those women around the planet who can't experience the freedom that we do, we must live our lives fully. We must be the God chicks on the earth. By influencing and loving the women in my expanded neighborhood, I am influencing other cultures. You can too. Just be faithful to be the God chick in your corner of the earth. You have a responsibility to be the most amazing you that you can be. There are women counting on you.

And the truth is, it's actually not just about you. Your actions will affect someone, whose actions will affect someone, whose actions will affect someone, whose actions will affect someone . . . and it just goes on and on. You have a responsibility to womanhood on the planet to be all that you were created to be. Do it for that young girl in Pakistan whose skin, because of the clothes she is required to wear, may never see the sun. Do it for the woman in the Middle East who is married to a man who continually abuses her and from whom she can't escape. Do it for the woman in central Africa who had to undergo female genital mutilation and so will not only never experience pleasure in intercourse, but will continually be plagued by infections. Don't hide behind fear or anger or a lack of confidence. The princess chick, the warrior chick, the champion chick, the friend chick, the party chick, the lover chick, and the whatever-it-takes chick all reside in you. You are woman, and you were put on the planet for "such a time as this." Now is your time. My job is to become the God chick I was created to be and to partner with man to see all that is good established on the earth. It's your job too. C'mon, you can do it! The world is counting on you.

Do what you can with what you have wherever you are.

—Theodore Roosevelt

the God chick

Proverbs 31:10–31 (AMPLIFIED)

A capable, intelligent (*champion chick*), and virtuous (*warrior chick*) woman—who is he who can find her?

She is far more precious than jewels and her value is far above rubies or pearls. (*princess chick*)

The heart of her husband trusts in her confidently and relies on and believes in her securely, so that he has no lack of [honest] gain or no need of [dishonest] spoil. (*lover chick*)

She comforts, encourages, and does him only good as long as there is life within her. (*lover chick*)

She seeks out wool and flax and works with willing hands to develop it.

She is like the merchant ships loaded with foodstuffs; she brings her household's food from a far country. (*whatever-it-takes chick*)

She rises while it is yet night and gets spiritual food for her household and assigns her maids their tasks. (*party chick*)

She considers a [new] field before she buys or accepts it [expanding prudently and not courting neglect of her present duties by assuming other duties]; with her savings [of time and strength] she plants fruitful vines in her vineyard. (*whatever-it-takes chick*)

She girds herself with strength [spiritual, mental, and physical fitness for her God-given task] and makes her arms strong and firm. (*champion chick*)

She tastes and sees that her gain from work [with and for God] is good; her lamp goes not out, but it burns on continually through the night [of trouble, privation, or sorrow, warning away fear, doubt, and distrust]. (*party chick*)

She lays her hands to the spindle, and her hands hold the distaff.

She opens her hand to the poor, yes, she reaches out her filled hands to the needy [whether in body, mind, or spirit]. (*whatever-it-takes chick*)

She fears not the snow for her family, for all her household are doubly clothed in scarlet. (*warrior chick*)

She makes for herself coverlets, cushions, and rugs of tapestry. Her clothing is of linen, pure and fine, and of purple [such as that of which the clothing of the priests and the hallowed cloths of the temple were made]. (*princess chick*)

Her husband is known in the [city's] gates, when he sits among the elders of the land. (*lover chick*)

She makes fine linen garments and leads others to buy them; she delivers to the merchants girdles [or sashes that free one up for service]. (*whatever-it-takes chick*)

Strength and dignity are her clothing and her position is strong and secure; she rejoices over the future [the day or time to come, knowing that she and her family are in readiness for it]! (*party chick*)

She opens her mouth in skillful and godly Wisdom, and on her tongue is the law of kindness [giving counsel and instruction]. (*party chick*)

She looks well to how things go in her household, and the bread of idleness [gossip, discontent, and self-pity] she will not eat. (*whatever-it-takes chick*)

Her children rise up and call her blessed [happy, fortunate, and to be envied]; and her husband boasts of and praises her, [saying], "Many daughters have done virtuously, nobly, and well [with the strength of character that is steadfast in goodness], but you excel them all! [Wow!] Charm and grace are deceptive, and beauty is vain [because it is not lasting], but a woman who reverently and worshipfully fears the Lord, she shall be praised! (*lover chick*)

Give her the fruit of her hands, and let her own works praise her in the gates [of the city]!

notes

CHAPTER 1

1. Cynthia Kersey, *Unstoppable* (Naperville, Ill: Sourcebooks, 1988), 47.
2. Oprah Winfrey "What I Know for Sure," *O, the Oprah Magazine,* September 2001, 310.

CHAPTER 3

1. James Strong, *The New Strong's Exhaustive Concordance of the Bible* (Nashville: Thomas Nelson Publishers, 1990), #2428.
2. Jessica deCourcy Hinds, International Women's Media Foundation, www.iwmf.org/courage.
3. Jan Yager, *Friendshifts: The Power of Friendship and How it Shapes Our Lives* (Stamford, Conn.: Hannacroix Creek Books, 1997), 117.

Chapter 4

1. *Sports Illustrated,* 11 August 1997, 55.
2. Mark Victor Hansen and Jack Canfield, *Chicken Soup for the Woman's Soul* (Deerfield Beach, Fla: Health Communications, 1996), 118.

Chapter 5

1. *O, the Oprah Magazine*, "Oprah Talks to Jane Fonda," September 2000.
2. James Hewitt, ed., *Illustrations Unlimited* (Wheaton, Ill.: Tyndale House, 1988), 338, citing Carl Rogers.
3. Ibid., 226.
4. Danielle Schlass, *Working Mother,* November 2000, 48.
5. Arlene F. Benedict, *The Joys of Friendship* (Kansas City: Andrews McMeel Publishing, 1997), 34, citing Dinah Maria Mulock Craik.
6. Terri Apter and Ruthellen Josselson, *Best Friends* (New York: Three Rivers Press, 1999), 147.
7. Susan L. Taylor, *In the Spirit* (New York: Harper Perennial, 1993), 9.
8. Apter and Josselson, *Best Friends,* 198.

Chapter 6

1. Arthur Lenihan, Ed., *The Best of Bits & Pieces,* (Chicago Ill.: Ragan Communications, Inc., 2000), 11.
2. Holly J. Morris, *U.S. News and World Report,* 3 September 2001, 49.

about the author

Holly Wagner is a popular speaker at conferences around the world, from Los Angeles to Australia, New Zealand, Canada, Scotland, and Wales. She always makes an impact on her audiences, and is known for her challenging, personable, and humorous style of addressing real-life issues. While dealing with situations that are important to us all, she gives powerful and tremendously impacting direction in the areas of building friendships, enhancing marriages, and developing character.

Crowned Miss Texas National Teenager at the age of eighteen, Holly went on to attend Duke University and Southern Methodist University. She then moved to Los Angeles working as an actress in TV, film, and modeling.

Her first book, *dumb things he does/dumb things she does*, published by Thomas Nelson Publishers, offers a humorous yet challenging approach to overcoming relationship obstacles and is garnering national and international attention. *she loves me/she loves me not,* published by Harper Collins, focuses on the relationships between women and offers insight on "Friendship Dos" and "Friendship Don'ts." Holly has appeared on television's *Fox Family Channel, The 700 Club, 100 Huntley Street, On Main Street, Good Morning Sydney,* the Australian *Beauty and the Beast,* and *Good Morning Australia,* speaking on effective relationships.

Her husband, Philip, is the Senior Pastor of The Oasis Christian Center, in Los Angeles, and together they lead this unique multiracial church that reaches the entertainers of Hollywood, families, and the business leaders in the community. Holly is one of the main teachers in the church and leads a dynamic women's ministry, encouraging women to be who God called them to be.

Holly loves all the parts of her life! She loves being Philip's wife and working on her marriage. She has a great time with her two children, Jordan and Paris, and is often seen cheering for their baseball and basketball teams!

For recreation, she enjoys spending time with her family and friends. She likes to exercise, having earned a black belt in karate, and goes scuba diving with her husband in some of the most beautiful spots in the world!

To contact Holly, please reach her through:

The Oasis Christian Center
4929 Wilshire Blvd. #750
Los Angeles, CA 90010
(323) 937-5433 x 114
www.oasisla.org

Management and availabilities contact:

Michael Smith & Associates
118 Medford Place
Franklin, TN 37064
Phone: (615) 794-5763
Fax: (615) 591-5694

thanks

—to my Father in heaven for my full and wonderful life.

—to Philip, for loving me all along the journey.

—to Jordan and Paris for just being awesome. I am so glad we are family.

—to the W.A.V.E. women, for walking with me on the God chick journey. Noriko and Joyce—I couldn't have done it without you!

—to my Oasis family. It is an honor to serve our King with you.

—to Bobbie, for your friendship, laughter, and inspiration. I am forever grateful you are in my life.

—to Shanelle, one of the most amazing God chicks I know. Thank you for your love—a gift beyond price.

Don't Let Me Get Me

Words and Music by Alecia Moore and Dallas Austin

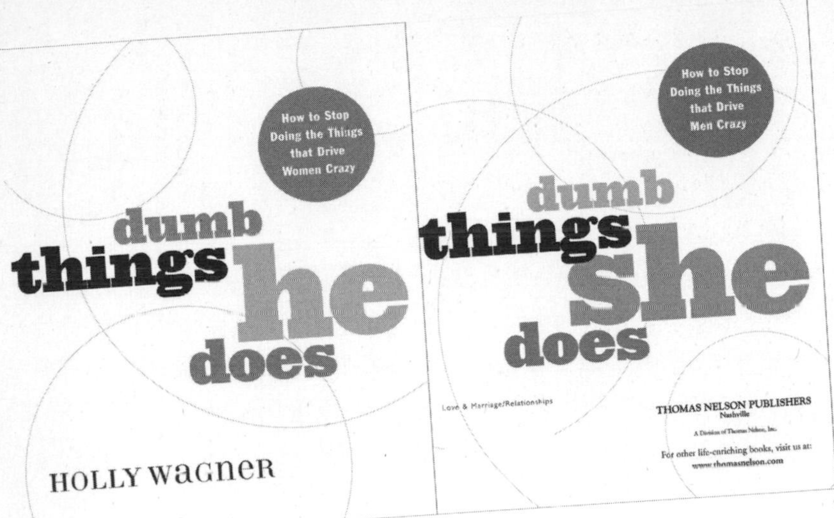

How to Stop Doing the Things that Drive Women Crazy
dumb things he does
HOLLY WAGNER
How to Stop Doing the Things that Drive Men Crazy
dumb things she does
Love & Marriage/Relationships
THOMAS NELSON PUBLISHERS
Nashville
For other life-enriching books, visit us at:
www.thomasnelson.com

AN EXPERT AT MAKING potentially complex issues easy to understand, Holly Wagner cuts to the chase and tells both men and women to "wise up"! Her playful yet challenging words encourage couples to appreciate their differences and make the most of them.

The dumb things men do—like failing to lead their families, avoiding growing up, and forgetting to keep courting their wives—are covered in the first third of the book. The reversed back third of the book features the dumb things women do, including disliking themselves, failing to demonstrate respect for their partners, and trying to "fix" men. The neutral center section presents the dumb things both sexes do, such as fighting in an unfair way, being unforgiving, and failing to understand the healthy differences between men and women.

ISBN: 0-7852-6520-1

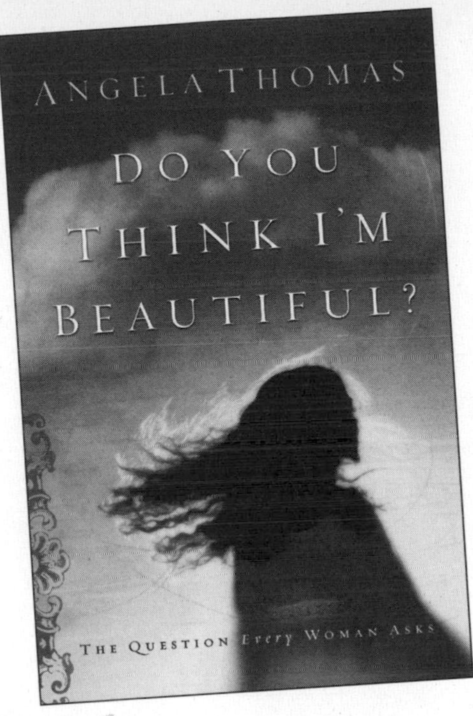

This book is for women who know, perhaps only deep in their hearts, that they need an answer to the question, "Do you think I'm beautiful?" Readers will come to understand that the question is uniquely feminine, placed there by the Creator to woo them to Himself. Along the way, women will learn about the distractions that can keep them from the One who calls them beautiful, what it takes to return to His embrace, and what delights await them there. Angela's skillful, moving writing style is peppered with warm and funny stories from her own life that readers will immediately identify with. And the practical Bible teaching Angela Thomas offers will help readers bridge the gulf between the life a woman longs for and the life she actually has.

ISBN: 0-7852-6355-1